Endorsements

The title says it all: *Spiritual Conversations: Creating and Sustaining Them without Being a Jerk.* Far too many well-meaning believers stumble over the basic principles of engagement with unbelievers. The relational, process-oriented approach Rohrmayer takes opens up practical skills we can use, as well as exploring the deeper principles at work in our approach to these conversations. If you want a book on the loaded topic of evangelism that is both helpful and real, read *Spiritual Conversations.* Rohrmayer knows of what he writes.

– Dr. Bob Logan,
Founder of CoachNet
www.coachnet.org

The great Apostle asked, "How are they going to hear without someone preaching?" The reality is that the eternal gospel goes forth to people from people. And, by experience, most people "hear" the gospel through a spiritual conversation not a sermon. This book empowers normal people to share the gospel through intentional conversations.

– Darrin Patrick
Lead Pastor of the Journey Church, St. Louis, Mo
Vice President of Acts 29 Network

Here is a book on "sensitive evangelism" written by a man who not only talks about it but does it. Gary Rohrmayer shows you how to find out where people are and to be used of God to help them move on what he calls their spiritual journey. Applying the principles in this book will transform you and your church.

– Robert Vajko
International Church Planting Consultant
The Evangelical Alliance Mission

Gary Rohrmayer has done it again. He keeps wearing me out in the right ways. I have been praying for God to make me into the evangelist that I once was, and *Spiritual Conversations* is part of how God is answering. Let's all do what Gary is telling us to do and get back into the game!

– Dr. Tom Nebel
Director of Church Planting
Converge Worldwide

Gary has a heart for lost people and knows how to talk to them and how to help you talk to them. I am planning on using this book as a valuable resource.

– Marcus Bigelow
President
Stadia: New Church Strategies
www.stadia.cc

Spiritual Conversations is simple and practical. It is not just another guy's theory on what might work in personal evangelism - I've watched this book in the making through Gary's life for years. He speaks from "in the trenches" training ... helping you move ahead with both diagnosis and prescription. I recommend this as great tool for any ministry or person that wants to effectively reach and help mature those God has put around them.

– Scott Ridout
Lead Pastor
Sun Valley Community Church
Gilbert, Arizona

It is refreshing to read a book when you know that the author does not just have a way with words but has lived out his message. I have known Gary Rohrmayer for almost a quarter of a century and his passion for evangelism and his love for those who are seeking Christ jump out from every page in this book. Not only will you gain a sound biblical and theological undergirding for the lost art of evangelism, Gary will also present clear and practical tools by which all of us can employ. Great Book! Don't leave home without it.

– Dr. Dwight Perry
Great Lakes Baptist Conference

Spiritual Conversations

Creating and Sustaining Them Without Being a Jerk

By Gary Rohrmayer

Published by ChurchSmart Resources

We are an evangelical Christian publisher committed to producing excellent products at affordable prices to help church leaders accomplish effective ministry in the areas of Church planting, Church growth, Church renewal and Leadership development.

For a free catalog of our resources call 1-800-253-4276.
Visit us at: www.ChurchSmart.com
For the author's complete contact information, turn to page 76.

ISBN: 1-889638-91-9
13 ISBN: 978-1-889638-91-1

Table of Contents

Dedication

To my father, Ronald Rohrmayer, who saw Jesus in spite of my weak attempts to share my faith.

Foreword

Joseph Bayly really must have been "out of his mind." His famous parable, *The Gospel Blimp* (Zondervan Publishing House, 1960) challenged long-held, well-established views of evangelism. The story centers on a sincere but misguided group of Christian couples. Burdened for the salvation of their beer drinking, non-church attending neighbors, they decided the lack of Gospel exposure was the issue. Inspiration arrived in the form of an advertising blimp flying overhead. They decided to deliver Gospel information to people in their town (including their neighbors) the same way. The blimp strategy soon evolved from advertising banners to air dropping Gospel tracts.

The story had a happy ending. Their neighbors came to Christ through relationships cultivated by two people from the group. The blimp idea didn't work. Patience and relationships did! After seeing the movie version of *The Gospel Blimp* (Gospel Films Distribution, 1967) you will wonder how Bayly could have lived through the 60's. Bayly was president of David C. Cook Publishers and wrote a monthly column for Eternity Magazine appropriately named "Out of My Mind."

Say goodbye to the blimp. Gospel information apart from a relationship with a real Christian will have limited results. The debate has twisted and turned for hundreds of years. Some say it is theological while others say it is methodological. Some say it is conversational while others say it is confrontational. We want to help people find and follow God . . . through a big time encounter with Jesus Christ via a real Christian. You may call it evangelism (insider language). Others call it proselytizing (outsider language). Whatever we call evangelism and regardless of our methodological approach we are all really hungry to see it happen.

We are eager for evangelistic results. That is good news and bad news for people far from God. What is worse than being lost? Being lost and having no one who is looking for you. Christians all over the planet at this minute are looking for people who are lost. That is good news. The bad news is that some don't share Christ at all. In addition, however, passion for the lost causes some people to share Christ poorly—and the end results is that people get pushed away. It takes time and it often takes conversations.

The story of the Ethiopian Eunuch (Acts 8) has inspired many sermons about evangelism. We all agree that God used Philip during a defining moment of the Ethiopian's spiritual journey. Most of us would also agree that "one size does not fit all" when it comes to our approach to people on a spiritual journey. So, what can we learn from the evangelistic episode that God fully intended for us to know about?

Philip approached the Eunuch because God led Him. He did not go into the meeting with a memorized script in hand. He started with a question. To want God's best for people far from Him is to care about where they are spiritually. Philip led with his ear, not with his mouth! He initiated a dialogue by asking a real (vs. canned) question: "When Philip ran up to it, he heard him reading the prophet Isaiah, and said, '*Do you understand what you're reading?*' 'How can I,' he said, 'unless someone guides me?' *So he invited Philip* to come up and sit with him" (Acts 8:30-32). Philip, by leading with his ear, was able to assess where the Eunuch was on his spiritual journey. But as important, the approach earned Philip permission to speak to the Eunuch further and informed him where to take the conversation.

Elmer Towns and I explained the significance of this principle,

> Traditionally, evangelizing has involved seeking to share the gospel as quickly and as thoroughly as possible with a potential believer and leading that person to pray to receive Christ on the spot. This method does not necessarily take into consideration the varying levels of spiritual awareness and attitude that are possible from person to person. One way to address this issue is to learn to be more sensitive to people and listen to them before jumping right into a prepared (or "canned") gospel presentation. [Elmer Towns and Ed Stetzer, *Perimeters of Light: Biblical Boundaries for the Emerging Church*, Chicago: Moody Press 2004, p. 148]

I illustrated the spiritual journey principle in the diagram on the following page. Although I believe conversion is a point in time experience, getting to that point and beyond is a step by step process. Apparent exceptions to the rule are seldom actual exceptions. People, conversations, and experiences are used by God to move a person to a defining moment with Christ.

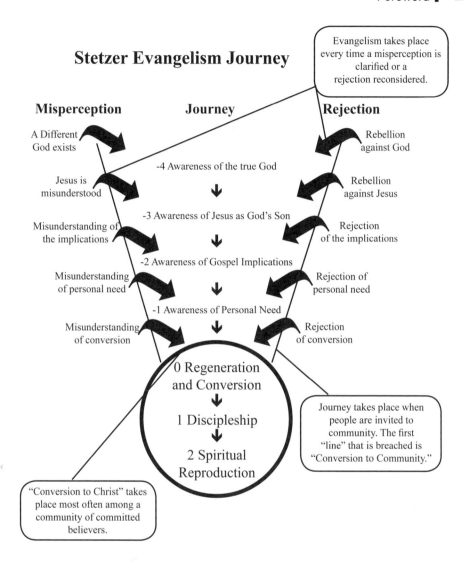

Stetzer Evangelism Journey

Evangelism takes place every time a misperception is clarified or a rejection reconsidered.

Misperception **Journey** **Rejection**

A Different God exists

Rebellion against God

-4 Awareness of the true God

Jesus is misunderstood

Rebellion against Jesus

-3 Awareness of Jesus as God's Son

Misunderstanding of the implications

Rejection of the implications

-2 Awareness of Gospel Implications

Misunderstanding of personal need

Rejection of personal need

-1 Awareness of Personal Need

Misunderstanding of conversion

Rejection of conversion

0 Regeneration and Conversion
1 Discipleship
2 Spiritual Reproduction

Journey takes place when people are invited to community. The first "line" that is breached is "Conversion to Community."

"Conversion to Christ" takes place most often among a community of committed believers.

Key truths must be processed about God, Jesus, the Gospel, personal need, and conversion during the journey. Obstacles to conversion are either misunderstanding or rejection of these key truths. The activity of God along the way moves people through the key truths.

Each curved arrow represents God encounters along the journey. For example, a person who has rejected God and who is living in rebellion can be challenged to live a different kind of life by a committed believer. In this context, the lost person can decide to consider the validity of a just God in conversation with their Christian friends. They may begin to believe that God is real and may then consider the claims of Christ. At some point, they begin to consider these things in community with believers.

The diagram illustrates two critical conversions. One conversion is temporal and one is eternal. The first conversion is the *conversion to community*. With few exceptions, people come to Christ after they have journeyed with other Christians—examining them and considering their claims. They can come into community at any point. Thus, the funnel-shaped lines (representing community) stretch all the way to the top of the diagram. At any point, a person can decide to begin a spiritual journey toward Christ.

The circle represents the Church. Church and Christian community must not be the same thing. Unbelievers can and should be invited into the community, but they are not part of the Church. A church is a body of believers. A person becomes part of the Church with the second and eternal conversion, the *conversion to Christ*.

The journey will not be the same for any individual, people group, worldview, or culture. For each individual, the misconceptions and reasons for rejecting the gospel may change, but each person must make the journey along the center column. By connecting people in community where they can hear and consider truths about Christ, they are more likely to make the journey of connecting with Christ.

Coaching is the buzz in the world of Christian leadership at the moment. Gary Rohrmayer was coaching before coaching was cool. The body of Christ has yet to understand the potential for multiplying leaders, disciples, through coaching. Gary is a practitioner. That comes through loud and clear through the pages of this book. He is a veteran evangelist, church planter, and pastor. But, in every sense of the word Rohrmayer is a coach. He has the heart of a coach in addition to the skills of a coach. He is optimistic about God's power to change people. He understands that every person is on a journey. They are waiting for someone to walk along side them and help them discover what God wants next.

Spiritual Conversations is more than a book about coaching. This book is much more than the latest in a long line of inspirational Christian books. *Spiritual Conversations* is a book about evangelism. You hold in your hand a practical tool. Plenty of good books will impress you and inspire you. God can use the book to empower you. Your greatest days engaging the harvest and raising leaders for the harvest are in the future.

Real evangelists love the harvesters more than the harvest. Even more, real love for the harvest is seen in love for the harvester. You know how you can see Jesus' love for the harvest? You can see Jesus' love for the harvest through His love and passion for harvesters. Notice His focus, "Then He said to His disciples, 'The harvest is abundant, but the workers are few. Therefore, pray to the Lord of the harvest to send out workers into His harvest'" (Matthew 9:37-38). This book will not only help you as a harvester. But this book will also help you help harvesters.

Imagine what it would be like if Christians took Gary's challenge in Chapter 7 to engage more people in spiritual conversations. Imagine if everyone who read this book applied the principles and agreed to tithe their time to engage their communities 5-10 hours a week. I see a new kind of evangelist being formed by God. This new kind of evangelist sees people on a journey and understanding the importance of walking along side them.

I can relate to what Gary described from his own life as being hit with a spiritual cannon ball in the gut all in the name of concern for his soul. I have been hit with a few cannon balls myself over the years. I must confess I have probably fired a few. I have met the jerks who witness with no concern for anything but another notch in the gun holster. I have, at times, been that jerk.

Jesus was an evangelist without being unnecessarily abrasive. We see Jesus, the evangelist, talking and listening. We hear Him asking questions and assessing. His love and care for people was clearly demonstrated. We never see Him in a hurry, yet we never see Him late. We watch Jesus turn as many people away from Him as He invited to follow. Many different people, situations, and points on a journey illustrated the approach of Jesus, the evangelist. Jesus could have used a blimp. He could have used the same presentation to every person. But Jesus was an evangelist. He used all the resources the Father had given Him to talk, listen, and advise people on their spiritual journey.

Now is the point where I am supposed to say this book is timely. I am more comfortable saying this book is overdue. I love lost people too much. More and better practices to reach lost people with the Gospel is always too late for the lost man, woman, or child who died today in my city.

Read this book with urgency. Wrestle with the key questions at the end of each chapter. Create new space in your life for people far from God. Make your goal, with the power of the Holy Spirit, to have more spiritual conversations in the next 90 days than you have ever had in your life. Then, play this book forward for the sake of the harvest. Tell your story and challenge others to follow your example. I am optimistic that God is up to something unusual. My heart is hungry to see God do something new and exciting. Imagine every man, woman, and child in every community in America with a fresh opportunity to see a real Christian and understand the Good News of Jesus Christ.

Say goodbye to the blimp! Gospel information apart from a relationship with a real Christian will have limited results. God plan is for you to relationally engage His mission for your town. Paul explained, "Now everything is from God, who reconciled us to Himself through Christ and gave us the ministry of reconciliation" (II Cor. 5:18).

– Dr. Ed Stetzer
President of LifeWay Research
Nashville, TN

Introduction – My Story

I had just moved into our new community with the intention of pioneering a new church. I was twenty-seven years old, equipped with a little experience, and a lot of raw passion. My wife Mary and I, along with our two little boys, were getting settled in, making all the necessary adjustments of new schools, new friends, finding part-time employment, etc. It was during this time that two men knocked at my door. They were both in suits so I immediately thought they were either Jehovah's Witnesses or Mormon Missionaries. But to my surprise the older of the two men said, "Hello, I'm a pastor from the local church in town and this is one of our members. We are just out welcoming new people to our town… do you have a few minutes?" I invited them in and they began to tell me about their church. In the midst of the conversation they asked me why our family had moved to town. I told them that I just graduated from Moody Bible Institute and was appointed by the Baptist General Conference (now Converge Worldwide) to plant a church in this city. The pastor sat up, looked me straight in the eye and with his deepest God voice said, "SO ARE YOU BORN AGAIN?!" As I remember that moment I can still feel the blast of those words pounding my chest. When I think about that moment the picture I see in my mind's eye is that of the old film clip of a man catching a cannonball as it is being shot out of the cannon!

> "Lord, let me never do that to someone else."

After I recovered from the blast of his spiritual cannon I replied with a definite yes. I began to share how Jesus had entered my life and radically changed the entire direction of my life, but from his reaction I think he doubted me. I never saw that pastor again, even during the ten years of serving in the same town together. The ironic thing was that we eventually built our new church facility less than one mile from his church.

When they both left I remember standing at the door just feeling dirty, as if I had been violated. I remember voicing a quick prayer, "Lord, let me never do that to someone else." From that moment on I resolved in my heart to never do that to anyone and I began asking God to show me how I could find out where someone was in their relationship with Jesus without violating them by being cruel, combative or callously confrontational. To put it simply…I was asking God to save me from being a jerk!

One night a year or so later it started to all come together. I was following up on a couple who had just attended our first Easter service. I was praying, "Lord show me how to discover where this couple is on their spiritual journey without offending them." I thought to myself…just ask them! After getting acquainted, I asked them, "Do you believe that everyone is on a spiritual journey?" To which they said, "Yes, of course." Then I began to paint a verbal picture of that journey. "There are basically two groups of people. There are *spiritual searchers* and *active followers* of Jesus. Within each group there are many different types of searchers and followers. There are those who casually approach spiritual things and there are those who are really intense in their search for true spirituality. On the other side there are those who have discovered the liberating joy of Christianity, who are either brand new in their walk with Jesus or growing deeper in their faith; maturing in their faith. But the thing that separates a spiritual searcher from a Christ follower is a *faith commitment.* A faith commitment is that defining moment when a person admits their spiritual need and discovers all that Jesus did for them and has said yes in their spirit to following Jesus as their risen Lord and only Savior."

> "Where would you say you are on your spiritual journey tonight?"

As I finished painting the picture before them I asked a simple but direct question, "Where would you say you are on your spiritual journey tonight?" The wife spoke first and said, "I'm just a brand new Christian" to which the husband gasped and replied, "If you're just a baby Christian then I am just a seeker and a casual one at that!"

I asked her to share with me about where and when she made her faith commitment. She said it was about a year earlier through a friend in the town they had just moved from. Then I followed up by asking her, "What is standing between you and becoming a mature follower of Jesus?" She said, "I just don't know enough about the Bible." I then extended an invitation to attend a new Bible study we were starting. I turned and asked the husband, "What is standing between you and making a faith commitment to Jesus?" He paused, thought awhile and said, "I guess I am just content. Things are going well right now. So I guess I am just casually seeking and bringing the family to church is enough right now." I encouraged him to continue bringing his family to church and to open himself to God's work in his life. I said, "We have many opportunities for you to get involved or to join a Bible study designed just for you. We call it Bible 101."

That night changed my life! I experienced a paradigm shift in my thinking. I moved from a mindset of decision-making evangelism to conducting a spiritual assessment. I went from doing the work for God to watching God at work. I changed from feeling the pressure of seeing people pray a forced prayer of repentance to experiencing the joy of seeing them discover their own barriers and issues that stood between them and Jesus. Don't get me wrong, there were many times I led people through a prayer of repentance who where crying out to be connected with God but there were many more occasions that I left people with a prescriptive plan for spiritual discovery or specific steps for moving them toward spiritual maturity.

> I moved from a mindset of decision-making evangelism to conducting a spiritual assessment.

A follow-up on that young couple I visited that fateful night: She got on a path of spiritual maturity, was placed in a mentoring relationship, followed Jesus' example in baptism and became a key leader in our children's ministry. Her husband kept coming, joined the set-up team, signed up for the Bible 101 course, joined the usher team, made a faith commitment, was placed in a mentoring relationship, followed Jesus' example in baptism and became a vital member on our building committee. Today they are active followers of Jesus.

Stop, Reflect, Discuss

- Have you ever had a spiritual cannonball shot into your chest?
- Have you ever shot a spiritual cannonball into someone?
- How does this story affect the way you will share your faith?
- How would you assess where a person is spiritually?

Chapter 1

Paradigm Shift

"Do you not say, 'Four months more and then the harvest'? I tell you, open your eyes and look at the fields! They are ripe for harvest ... I sent you to reap what you have not worked for. Others have done the hard work, and you have reaped the benefits of their labor."
— John 4:35, 38

A paradigm shift is when something so revolutionary happens, that it shakes up not only the way we view our world but also the way we fundamentally operate in our world. Thomas Kuhn popularized the term 'paradigm shift' in his writing in the early 1960's. He explained that advancements in science were not evolutionary but more a "series of peaceful interludes punctuated by intellectually violent revolutions" that caused "one conceptual world view to be replaced by another view." [1]

Over the last twenty-five years my view of evangelism has been radically replaced with another perspective. I have seen, felt and experienced a paradigm shift in my attitude towards the practice of evangelism. Here are a few personal observations of how this shift has taken place over the last twenty-five years.

Moving from Event Driven to Process Oriented

I think the confusion between the event of conversion and the process of evangelism was generated by the majority of evangelism training being centered around leading someone in a prayer of repentance, while little has been offered in identifying the steps a person takes in moving toward or away from Christ or with Christ in a life of discipleship. In the mid-80's I discovered the writings of Dr. James F. Engel and his Engel's scale (see illustration) while at the same time I was introduced to Willow Creek Community Church's Seven Step Philosophy of Ministry Strategy. 1) Build a relationship with others outside the family. 2) Share verbal witness with them. 3) Bring them to an outreach event. 4) Help them participate in our midweek services. 5) Get them involved in a small group. 6) Encourage them to serve in the church according to their spiritual gifts and 7) Teach them how to practice healthy stewardship of their resources to build the kingdom.[2]

The combination of these ideas helped me make the shift from event focused evangelism to more of a relational process oriented approach. It is an approach grounded in the fact that God is drawing people to himself (John 6:44) and that he invites me to be part of His great redemptive process (Acts 1:8). Making this shift brings such freedom in my evangelistic efforts because it means that every conversation, every discovery and every decision, whether big or small, is a glorious victory that reveals the Holy Spirit's work in the lives of those he has brought and is bringing across my path.

Engel's Scale of Evangelism	
-10	Awareness of the supernatural
-9	No effective knowledge of Christianity
-8	Initial awareness of Christianity
-7	Interest in Christianity
-6	Awareness of basic facts of the Gospel
-5	Grasp of implications of the Gospel
-4	Positive attitude to the Gospel
-3	Awareness of personal need
-2	Challenge and decision to act
-1	Repentance and faith
0	A Disciple is born!
+1	Evaluation of decision
+2	Initiation into the church
+3	Become part of the process of making other disciples
+4	Growth in understanding of the faith
+5	Growth in Christian character
+6	Discovery and use of gifts
+7	Christian life-style
+8	Stewardship of resources
+9	Prayer
+10	Openness to others/Effective sharing of faith and life

Moving from a Combative Approach to Attractive Posture

Most of the evangelism training I experienced in school and in seminars was apologetically driven. Don't get me wrong, it is biblical to be prepared. Peter wrote, "Always be prepared to give an answer to everyone who asks you to give the reason for the hope that you have." (I Peter 3:15) Yet all too often I missed the two key concepts around this portion of Scripture 1) Lordship - *"But in your hearts set apart Christ as Lord."* It is making sure that our lives are aligned with Christ through personal purity, through confession of all known sin and being filled with the Holy Spirit. Allowing Christ to reign in our lives will turn controversial information into transformational truth. 2) Rapport - *"But do this with gentleness and respect, keeping a clear conscience, so that those who speak maliciously against your good behavior in Christ may be ashamed of their slander."* (I Peter 3:15-16) Rapport is that emotional bond or friendly relationship between people based on mutual respect, trust and care. Lordship and rapport are the keys that save us from being combative and make us more attractive in spiritual conversations. One of my students in a seminary course I was teaching agreed with my premise in this point but commented that there are times when you just need to confront people with the truth. At that point I so wanted to pull a "Dr. Phil" and say, "Tell me, how's that working for ya?" But that would have been combative! So, instead I asked him to study Jesus' interactions with people. The only times he was combative was with the religious elite who distracted people from the truth of God and put up needless man-made barriers that kept them from experiencing the transformational truth of the kingdom. (Matthew 23; Luke 19:45-46)

> **Lordship and rapport are the keys that save us from being combative and make us more attractive in spiritual conversations.**

God makes his gospel attractive through his people. Paul in his letter to Titus encourages this young leader to instruct the church on the island of Crete to have "sound doctrine" (Titus 2:1); to think correctly and to behave correctly. He gives Titus specific instructions to every segment of the church, older men and women (Titus 2:3-4), younger men and women (Titus 2:5-6) and even slaves (Titus 2:9-10). He ends his exhortation with these words "… so that in every way they will make the teaching about God our Savior attractive." (Titus 2:10)

He asked those who lived in the worst of circumstances, 'slavery,' to live out the power of the gospel in a way that makes the gospel attractive. That produces a desire within a person they may rub shoulders with and encourages them to say, "I want what *you* have." God makes his gospel attractive through people…that is the point of the gospel; it is transformative in nature. Paul drives this point further in the next few verses, "For the grace of God that brings salvation has appeared to all men. It teaches us to say "no" to ungodliness and worldly passions, and to live self-controlled, upright and godly lives in this present age, while we wait for the blessed hope—the glorious appearing of our great God and Savior, Jesus Christ, who gave himself for us to redeem us from all wickedness and to purify for himself a people that are his very own, eager to do what is good." (Titus 2:11-14) The essence of the gospel message is that it is transformational, it changes one's behavior, it revolutionizes one's motivations and it makes God's message attractive to a world craving truth and light. Jesus said, "You are the light of the world. A city on a hill cannot be hidden. Neither do people light a lamp and put it under a bowl. Instead they put it on its stand, and it gives light to everyone in the house. In the same way, let your light shine before men, that they may see your good deeds and praise your Father in heaven." (Matthew 5:14-16)

As people allow the Lordship of Christ to guide their heart and as they build a strong emotional connection with those in their lives, the gospel becomes something that the people in their world are *drawn to* and not *repelled from.*

Moving from a Memorized Monologue to a Meaningful Dialogue

There has been a profound shift, moving from giving a memorized sales pitch to a meaningful two-way conversation. In my early days of ministry I was driven by decision theology (we had to report something to our supporters). Then one fateful night I was hearing a report from a chaplain in a prison ministry who said, "I have seen thousands of men make decisions for Jesus in my ministry" to which a wise, older woman asked, "But what about discipling these men? How does that happen?" His response was, "That's the Lord's business, I will just have to trust him with that." I opened my Bible and read the great commission in Matthew 28:19 where Jesus said, "go make disciples" not "go make decisions!" Monologues are like decision based theology, they are neat and tidy. Dialogues are like disciple-making, they are messy and unpredictable. Learning to see God at work in the messes is challenging and exciting. Monologues take a little practice and can come across as impersonal. Dialogues take faith, patience and love.

> Monologues are like decision based theology, they are neat and tidy. Dialogues are like disciple-making, they are messy and unpredictable.

All too often we preach rather than discuss. To interact relationally one needs to listen more than he or she speaks, one needs to get beyond the surface conversations to the heart of the matter. Meaningful dialogue will only occur when trust is established. If we are selling anything, it is trust and trust alone! In every conversation we have people ask themselves these questions, "Why should I trust this person?" "Why should I trust what they are saying?" "What makes them credible?"

Michael Simpson has built a great evangelistic model off Seth Godin's groundbreaking book, *Permission Marketing*. He takes Godin's key concepts and builds a model that he calls Permission Evangelism. Here is his definition: "The purpose of permission in evangelism is to create trust, get around the legal and social barriers to discussing your faith and most importantly, to discern the leading of the Holy Spirit in someone's life."[3]

Moving from a Short-term Contact to a Long-term Relationship

A short-term mentality works through this type of sequence: 1) Presentation 2) Decision 3) Assimilation. A long-term mentality operates with this sequence in mind: 1) Belonging 2) Believing 3) Becoming. On an individual and corporate level the church is learning to love and accept people where they are at on their journey, along with providing opportunities and experiences for them to engage relationally with other Christians, along with exploring the implications of Christ's teachings. I am a big proponent of the concept that Christianity is more "caught than taught" and that a person's

Short Term	Long Term
Presentation	Belonging
Decision	Believing
Assimilation	Becoming

meaningful involvement in the process is critical to his or her experiencing the power of the gospel in his or her life. This meaningful involvement takes time and persevering love. There was a season in our church where several men came to faith through their engagement in our set-up team. It was a place in our church where they could make an instant impact and rub shoulders with other men of faith. Over time we saw them move towards Christ by attending retreats, men's events and small groups. They eventually came to faith and moved into a life of discipleship. Actually, before we moved into our permanent building, the gentleman leading the team was someone who had walked in the door about four years earlier as a sincere spiritual searcher who experienced the transforming power of the gospel.

These four shifts have touched me to the core of my being. They have revolutionized my attitude toward evangelism to where I am more sensitive to the Holy Spirit in my conversations and I celebrate the mini decisions and the little steps that people make towards Jesus and his message. So no, I don't see the end product of a successful evangelistic contact as seeing people pray a prayer of repentance but I see the end product as helping them take the next step on their spiritual journey.

Stop, Reflect, Do

- What evidence do you see in the shift from event to process in your spiritual conversations?
- When was Jesus ever combative with anyone but the Pharisees?

- How are you maintaining long-term relationships in your life with those who are spiritually searching?

Chapter 2

Seven Reasons
for the Shift

"No one can come to me unless the Father who sent me draws him,
and I will raise him up at the last day."
– John 6:44

Making the paradigm shift from event to process is an exciting spiritual journey. Moving from the combative to the attractive route is just plain liberating. Shifting from a meaningless monologue to a meaningful dialogue becomes a relational adventure. Changing from a short-term interaction to a long-term relationship is stretching and life-changing.

So, why is making this revolutionary shift so imperative? Here are seven reasons:

1. We live in a world where God is always at work all around us.

Leonard Sweet once said, "Postmodern evangelism is recognizing that God is already at work in people's lives before we arrived on the scene and that our role is helping people to see how God is present and active in their lives, calling them home." Leonard Sweet perfectly describes what I like to call conducting a 'spiritual assessment.' A **Spiritual Assessment** is simply identifying how deeply the work of the Holy Spirit is active in the lives of individuals along with helping them discover and embrace that work of God in their lives. Grasping this foundational truth and understanding how God is at work all around you will grant you a greater sense of confidence to enter into more spiritual conversations. Here is a short list of the ways God is at work in our world.

How is God at work in our world?

- He is convicting the world, "When he comes, he will convict the world of guilt in regard to sin and righteousness and judgment: in regard to sin, because men do not believe in me; in regard to righteousness, because I am going to the Father, where you can see me no longer; and in regard to judgment, because the prince of this world now stands condemned." (John 16:8)

- He is drawing people to Himself, "No one can come to me unless the Father who sent me draws him, and I will raise him up at the last day." (John 6:44)

- He is seeking the lost, "For the Son of Man came to seek and to save what was lost." (Luke 19:10)

- He is calling people to follow Him, "If anyone would come after me, he must deny himself and take up his cross daily and follow me." (Luke 9:23)

- He is opening hearts, "The Lord opened her heart to respond to Paul's message." (Acts 16:14)

- He is calling believers into a love relationship with Him, "Here I am! I stand at the door and knock. If anyone hears my voice and opens the door, I will come in and eat with him, and he with me." (Revelation 3:20)

- He is sending forth His message through His messengers, "As the Father has sent me, I am sending you." (John 20:21) "But you will receive power when the Holy Spirit comes on you; and you will be my witnesses in Jerusalem, and in all Judea and Samaria, and to the ends of the earth." (Acts 1:8)

J.I. Packer, in his classic work, *Evangelism and the Sovereignty of God*, answers the question, "If God is sovereign in the work of the salvation of the souls of humanity then wouldn't evangelism be pointless?"

> "Some fear that belief in the sovereign grace of God leads to the conclusion that evangelism is pointless, since God will save His elect anyway, whether they hear the gospel or not. This, as we have seen, is a false conclusion based on a false assumption. But now we must go further, and point out that the truth is just the opposite. So far from making evangelism pointless, the

sovereignty of God in grace is the one thing that prevents evangelism from being pointless. For it creates the possibility – indeed, the certainty – that evangelism will be fruitful. Apart from it, there is not even a possibility of evangelism being fruitful. Were it not for the sovereign grace of God, evangelism would be the most futile and useless enterprise that the world has ever seen, and there would be no more complete waste of time under the sun than to preach the Christian gospel." (pg 106)

If people are going to increase their spiritual conversations they must be equipped to do a spiritual assessment; this will save them from needless arguments, unfruitful misunderstandings and wasted energy. If every pastor, lay leader and active follower of Christ was taught how to assess the work of the Holy Spirit in the lives of those who come along their path, I believe we would increase our number of spiritual conversations dramatically.

2. We live in an age where spiritual seeking is rampant in our culture.

Spiritual seeking is rampant in our culture. In researching the role of faith in Americans' lifestyles, researcher George Barna asked people if they consider themselves "deeply spiritual."

- Percentage of those Barna classified as born-again Christians who considered themselves "deeply spiritual": 79%

- Percentage of those Barna did not classify as born-again Christians who considered themselves "deeply spiritual": 46% (source: www.barna.org)

This means that nearly 1 out of 2 people you meet see themselves as deeply spiritual, yet with all this increased spirituality comes a lot of confusion. The following is how Steven Van Zandt, a rock 'n' roll guitarist who was a member of Bruce Springsteen's E Street Band, described his spirituality, "I am a reformed Taoist, part-time Buddhist, Hindu, animist, pagan, Jewish mystic and Christian. I always got along great with priests and rabbis and mullahs and gurus, even though I spend most of my life constructively criticizing them."

For years I wrestled with the apparent contradiction between what Scripture said and what I witnessed in our culture. I read Romans 3:11, which says, "…there is no one who understands, no one who seeks God…" Then I saw a world hungry for spirituality. It has invaded every segment of society from the boardroom to the bedroom, from the top notch business schools to ongoing medical studies on the effects of prayer in the healing process!

It all came together one day when I read R.C. Sproul's comment on Romans 3:11. He said, "People don't seek God, they are only seeking the benefits of God." (Source: *Table Talk Magazine,* www.ligonier.org)[1] People seek love, joy, peace and happiness but they don't seek a holy, transcendent, glorious and majestic God who is to be feared, loved and awed. This discovery led me to the conclusion that my job is to point them to the God who loves them, to Jesus who died for them and to the Holy Spirit who is at work in their lives.

3. We live in age where self-discovery is very important and can be very empowering.

We live in an age where people chaff at being told what to do! From the anti-establishment era of the sixties to the self-help wave of the nineties. There is a deep ownership that takes place when one discovers the work of God in his or her life.

George G. Hunter III observes in his book, *How to Reach Secular People,* "Effective communicators do not try to do all the communicating. They know that the faith is 'more caught than taught,' that a person's meaningful involvement can do its own communicating, and that involvement helps people discover the faith for themselves." (pg. 99-100)[2]

I like the example of Zacchaeus in Luke 19:1-10. Zacchaeus was a true seeker who went to great lengths to see Jesus. He had personal ownership of his journey but then came into one of the greatest discoveries a convert can make, that Jesus was seeking him all along. When a person discovers that God loves him or her enough to draw him or her to Himself it is very empowering and transformational. What did Zacchaeus declare when the sincerity of his faith was questioned? He said, "Look, Lord! Here and now I give half of my possessions to the poor, and if I have cheated anybody out of anything, I will pay back four times the amount." (Luke 19:8)

4. We live in an age of implementation not just information.

The nineties have been known as the information age. Our access to the World Wide Web with complete libraries on it is overwhelming at times. Many experts say that the new millennium is the implementation age. How do we apply all the information that is bombarding our lives? This is revealed in the coaching craze that is running across the country as we are seeing: executive coaching; financial coaches; personal training coaching; coaches for pastors, church planting and missionaries.

Sometimes people just need a little help in implementing the truth they are wrestling with. Take for example the gentleman who had been coming to a Bible study I was leading. For three weeks he was asking every question you could imagine…then he started repeating his questions, again. I knew then he was ready! God was preparing him for that moment he had no more excuses. He needed someone to guide him through this needed step of faith. As a group we gathered around him, held hands and prayed that he would respond to God's work in his life by entrusting his life to the care and control of Jesus Christ. As we finished praying he voiced a sincere prayer of faith acknowledging Jesus as his only Savior and leader of his life. Today, he is growing in his faith and serving his Lord on a worship team in a local church.

5. We live in a world where people are craving love and gentle guidance.

In Ed Stetzer's book, *Lost and Found*, he discovered that 89% of 20-29 year olds would be willing to listen to someone share their Christian beliefs. This percentage decreased to 75% of those 30 or older (pg 55).[3] According to this research, 9 out of 10 young adults in their 20's are willing to engage in a spiritual conversation as well as 7 out of 10 adults over 30! Let that sink in for a minute! The opportunities for meaningful spiritual conversations are overwhelming. It is imperative that we learn how to make the most of these opportunities in a loving and gentle way that guides a person into truth, not forcefully confronting them. If we are to give spiritual guidance we must lovingly help people identify the barriers they are facing and gently give them the next steps toward spiritual discovery or maturity.

I walked into a couple's home one night following up on their attendance to our Newcomers Class. After we sat down, this professional businesswoman started the conversation by saying, "I just want to know if this church is going to accept us because we are not married, we are living together and I am pro-choice in my beliefs."

I calmly responded by saying, "We believe everyone is on a spiritual journey and if I told you that you need to obey my moral code it still won't make you a follower of Jesus. But let me say this, don't be surprised that when you move closer and closer to Jesus and come under the authority of his teaching that your values will start to change." She said, "You know I don't know much about the Bible but I would like to." I asked if they would be willing to host a Bible 101 class in their home and they both agreed. Within a few weeks we had 10-12 people just like them study the Bible in their home. Within six months they both embraced Jesus as their only Savior and risen Lord. They both entered into a mentoring relationship, followed Jesus' example in baptism and I had the privilege of performing their wedding a little more than a year from that conversation. I believe there are couples like this all around us, craving someone to gently and confidently guide them into the truth of the gospel.

6. We live in a world where people need relationships that are cultivated and sustained.

A new study by sociologists at Duke University and the University of Arizona has revealed that Americans' circle of close confidants has shrunk dramatically in the past two decades and the number of people who say they have no one with whom to discuss important matters has more than doubled.[1]

So much of our evangelism and visitation ministry is void of relationship. We are in and out of people's lives in a rapid pace and rarely move beyond the superficial. In conducting a spiritual assessment one establishes a point of reference that builds a relationship not ends one. On many occasions I followed up with individuals and asked this very natural question, "So where are you now on your spiritual journey?" This has given me many opportunities to cultivate spiritual soil while deepening the relationship. The mission that Jesus invites us to participate in is primarily a relational one in nature. Our ability to sustain our relationship in a meaningful way will have a direct impact on our missional fruitfulness.

7. We live in an age where believers are educated well beyond their level of obedience.

Many churches look at discipleship as dispensing knowledge. If we pump enough Bible into their brains then we have done our jobs but Jesus sees discipleship as a training process. He said, "...teaching them to obey everything I have commanded." (Matthew 28:20) Jesus is interested in not only dispensing truth but in the shaping of our values. Shaping the values of another person is messy and takes patience, love and time. It takes hard conversations. It takes specific encouragement. It takes a watchful eye. It takes time, commitment and sacrifice. This is where a consistent plan for conducting spiritual assessments in a local church will assist believers to continually live a life of self-awareness and self-surrender which will lead to the shaping of one's core values and to missional fruitfulness.

I was conducting an Evangelism and Discipleship Seminar in a local church and was describing the spiritual journey to a group of church leaders. One man who had been a faithful member in his church for a number of years asked, "How does one move from growing in community to living missionally?" I paused for a second when a woman from the other side of the room stood up and said, "That's why we are here Joe! That's why we are here!" This group of people wanted to move to the next level in their faith journey. They were tired of just being the *church for each other.* They came with a hunger to be the *church to the lost* world right at their door steps. They wanted practical ways and effective tools to help them create and sustain spiritual conversations along with tools for effectively mentoring people in the life of discipleship.

In recent years I have started to do consulting with established churches as well as with new churches. In any consultation one must spend time listening and gathering information to make a healthy diagnosis before offering a plan for health and growth. If pastors would make a one-year goal of taking every board member, every member, and every visitor through a personal spiritual assessment not only would they discover the barriers of growth in their people, they would be on their way to overcoming the barriers of growth in their whole congregation.

Embracing the Shift

Throughout high school I played football and one of the things I hated was to be on the sidelines...I wanted to be in the game...I wanted to be in the action. If I could have played every minute...that is what I would have done. Sitting on the bench was miserable. I meet many spiritual leaders that want to and desire to get into the game of evangelistic effectiveness. They are tired of sitting on the bench; they are tired of hearing the stories of others and desperately desire to have their own stories. In my humble opinion that will never happen until they embrace the shift that has taken place over the last twenty-five years and move away from the tools and techniques that worked 30-40 years ago. If they don't they will be sitting on the sidelines frustrated, watching the game pass by right in front of them.

Stop, Reflect, Discuss

- What are some of the ways that you can identify that God is at work in your relationships?
- How can we use the rampant spiritual confusion as an opportunity to engage people in meaningful conversations?
- Where have you seen the power of self-discovery at work in your own life?
- Discuss the difference between an evangelist and a spiritual coach.
- Do you agree with the assumption that people are craving gentle, spiritual guidance?

Chapter 3

The Person of
Peace Principle

"When you enter a house, first say, 'Peace to this house.' If a man of peace is there, your peace will rest on him; if not, it will return to you."
– Luke 10:5

In my opinion most of the evangelistic training that is available is geared toward those who are non-receptive and even hostile to the gospel. The majority of the training that I have experienced has been apologetically driven, almost taking on a defensive posture. Don't get me wrong, I believe we should all be trained and be able to give a reason for what we believe. But I am convinced there needs to be more offensive training on how to go out and identify those who have a higher degree of receptivity to the gospel message.

One of these offensive measures is the "Man of Peace Principle" or the "Person of Peace Principle" which is a scriptural concept Jesus taught his disciples as he sent them out on a mission. In Luke 10:5-6 Jesus said, "When you enter a house, first say, `Peace to this house.' If a man of peace is there, your peace will rest on him; if not, it will return to you. Stay in that house, eating and drinking whatever they give you, for the worker deserves his wages. Do not move around from house to house." (Luke 10:5-6 NIV)

Let us break this passage down. The context is the second mission that Jesus used to train his ever expanding group of followers. The first mission was with the twelve in Luke 9:1-6. Jesus appointed the twelve (Luke 6:12) as apostles, he empowered them, gave them some general instruction and sent them out on their first mission. After they were finished he received a follow up report (Luke 9:10).

This second mission is now expanded to seventy-two disciples who accepted the invitation to follow Jesus and who are now being sent out on a training mission. The Person of Peace Principle is the heart of Jesus' training instructions. Here is a brief overview of the principles Jesus used to equip his followers:

1. God is at work and opportunities abound. – "The harvest is plentiful…" (Luke 10:2)
2. Pray specifically. – "Ask the Lord of the harvest, therefore, to send out workers into his harvest field." (Luke 10:2) Pray not for converts but recipients who will take the message further.
3. Embrace the risks involved. – "Go! I am sending you out like lambs among wolves." (Luke 10:3)
4. Travel light and don't get sidetracked – "Do not take a purse or bag or sandals; and do not greet anyone on the road." (Luke 10:4)
5. Find receptive workers: Men and women of peace – (Luke 10:5-6)
6. Stay with them – "Stay in that house, eating and drinking whatever they give you, for the worker deserves his wages. Do not move around from house to house. When you enter a town and are welcomed, eat what is set before you." (Luke 10:7-8)
7. Exercise compassion through meeting physical needs – "Heal the sick who are there." (Luke:10:9)
8. Proclaim the message of the Kingdom – "…tell them, 'The kingdom of God is near you.'" (Luke 10:9)
9. Don't take rejection personally. – "He who listens to you listens to me; he who rejects you rejects me; but he who rejects me rejects him who sent me." (Luke 10:16)
10. Embrace the joy of the mission. – "Blessed are the eyes that see what you see. For I tell you that many prophets and kings wanted to see what you see but did not see it, and to hear what you hear but did not hear it." (Luke 10:23-24)

Jesus not only instructed the seventy-two to pray specifically for more workers to enter the harvest but He also gave them a tool for discovering those workers. The Person of Peace Principle is that tool. This shift in our thinking is significant. We are not called to find converts but to find potential workers who will take the message further. These potential workers are not just responsive to the message, but also the messengers, and they leverage their influence within their community to become conduits through whom the message of the kingdom will be spread.

Let's break down this principle: Jesus said, "When you enter a house, first say, 'Peace to this house.'" It was a common and simple greeting used throughout the Old Testament (Genesis 43:23, Judges 6:23;19:20; I Sam 25:6) and was also used by Jesus himself (Luke 24:36; John 20:19,21,26). The key here isn't in the blessing itself but the critical factor is in who is pronouncing that blessing and in whose authority that blessing is given. The seventy-two were messengers of peace, who where commissioned by the Prince of Peace, to go out under His authority and with His power. In this context, when a person welcomed and received the disciples into his home, he displayed a great level of receptivity and provided an opportunity for God's peace to rest on him. If he did not welcome or receive the disciples this meant that God was not at work in that household.

Do you have friends, family, neighbors who know that you are follower of Jesus and are very welcoming and open to a relationship with you? This is a strong indicator of the work of God in their lives and should not be taken lightly but should be nurtured carefully and gently. This is why Jesus instructed them to stay and live life with those who were receptive to them because it meant that they were open to the message they were bringing.

There are four identifiable marks of a Person of Peace. The first mark of a Person of Peace is that he or she is *receptive to the messenger.* We see this in the life of Jesus. The woman at the well was open to a conservation with Jesus (John 4:14-17), the demoniac came and sought out Jesus (Mark 5:1), Zaccheus climbed a tree to get a glimpse of Jesus (Luke 19:4). We also see this in the life of the Apostles, the Ethiopian eunuch was open and welcoming to Philip (Acts 9). Cornelius eagerly welcomed and invited Peter into his home (Acts 10). Lydia welcomed Paul and Silas into her home (Acts 16) as did the Philippian jailer who sought out Paul and Silas and brought them into his home (Acts 16).

The second mark of a Person of Peace is that he or she is *responsive to the message*. The woman at the well responded to Jesus' words with honest questions (John 4). The demoniac responded in obedience to Jesus' words (Mark 5). Zaccheus responded by proclaiming his faith and through public repentance (Luke 19). The Ethiopian eunuch desired to be baptized (Acts 9). Cornelius shared his vision with others (Acts 10). Lydia received Paul's message and shared the message with her household (Acts 16:14). The Philippian jailer received the word of the Lord and shared the message with his household (Acts 16: 31-34).

The third mark of a Person of Peace is that he or she has a ***known reputation in his or her community whether positive or negative.*** The woman at the well had a negative reputation in her community and her transformation touched the whole community (John 4). The demoniac was known and observed by people (Mark 5:15). Zaccheus was the chief of tax collectors, an influential position in his community (Luke 19:1-9). The Ethiopian eunuch held a high governmental position in his country (Acts 8:24). Lydia was a prominent businesswoman and influential over her household (Acts 16:13) and the Philippian jailer was a high ranking official and influential member of his household (Act 16:34). Each of the individuals impacted their sphere of influence and became conduits of grace to the people who knew them.

The fourth mark of a Person of Peace is that he or she is ***highly relational***. They possess that natural ability to connect easily with people and to connect others into their sphere of relationship. The woman at the well was very relational in a negative way (John 4: 39-42). The demoniac shared his story with his family and throughout the region (Mark 5:19-20). Zaccheus was well connected throughout his community as a chief tax collector (Luke 19:2). Lydia and the Philippian jailer saw the gospel touch their entire households (Acts 16:14, 34).

How does one discern if a Person of Peace is in his or her life? Here are a few things to look for:

1. Did they receive you openly into their lives knowing that you are a follower of Jesus?
2. Are they open to spiritual conversations? Meaning, you can dialogue with them about spiritual issues without them shutting down emotionally.
3. Are they willing to look into the Scriptures with a curious spirit and not a critical one?
4. Do they have influence with others? Are they in a position of influence over their family, friends and within the community?
5. Is their home a hub of activity for the neighborhood and extended family?
6. Do they have the ability to introduce new people into their sphere of influence effectively?
7. Do they have a natural ability of including and bringing others to small groups, events or worship services?

One Person of Peace I discovered in our ministry was a young businessman who grabbed me after one of our worship services and said, "I need someone to teach me the Bible" and then gave me his business card and left. A clear indication of being receptive!   Interestingly, I was praying that week for God to lead me to someone that I could work with one-on-one.

I followed up with a phone call and scheduled a lunch appointment with him. We talked and I assessed where he was on his spiritual journey and asked if he would be open to meeting weekly for Bible study. He was very responsive and we began studying the Bible together on a weekly basis.

During one of our weekly meetings, he said, "I wish I had you in my hip pocket because you have all the answers and I keep getting into all these spiritual conversations and feel like I am just fumbling around all the time." I responded, "How many people are we talking about?" He said, "I don't know…10-20."

I responded, "Do you think you could gather all these people together for a Question & Answer session at your house? They can ask me any question they want related to faith, religion, Jesus and the Bible." He said, "You mean we can play 'stump the chump'?" I said, "Sure." Then I realized I was the "chump" in that equation! I loved being a "chump" for Jesus! Within two weeks he had five to six couples at his home. I answered all their questions, handed them a spiritual journey guide and asked if they would like to meet next week. The very next week a young woman who attended came up to me with the spiritual journey guide I had given her, which was all marked up and said, "Something happened to me this week, I think I had a spiritual epiphany! I read through this journey guide, I answered all the questions on the back and I prayed the prayer that was provided. I haven't been the same since!" Over the next six to eight months every one of these couples discovered the liberating joy of following Jesus. This one Person of Peace along with his natural relational skills, was able to bring me into his circle of relationships. Today, this gentleman employs 1% of the population in the community where he lives and touches hundreds of people through his positive testimony.

Stop, Reflect & Discuss:

- Are you praying to discover the Person of Peace in your life?
- Have you ever encountered a Person of Peace?
- What would you do if God put a Person of Peace in your life?
- What are some ways you can discover the Person of Peace in your community?

Chapter 4
Spiritual Conversation Tool

"Always be prepared to give an answer to everyone who asks you to give the reason for the hope that you have. But do this with gentleness and respect, keeping a clear conscience, so that those who speak maliciously against your good behavior in Christ may be ashamed of their slander."
— (I Peter 3:15-16)

If we are going to contextualize the Person of Peace Principle within our culture we need to answer the question: What is the 'Peace to this house' greeting, statement or question for your cultural context? This is a critical missional principle for anyone who wants to increase their number of spiritual conversations and evangelistic fruitfulness. In my practice as an evangelism coach for pastors, church planters and missionaries this discovery is a vital piece of the coaching experience. When I was in the Philippines working with pastors and church planters helping them increase the evangelistic effectiveness, I would spend forty-eight hours with each pastor, living in their home and walking side by side with them in their ministry day. During the first thirty-six hours I would just build a relationship with them and their family, observing them in their ministry environment, by attending bible studies, going on visitation with them, prayer walks in their area, etc. During this time I began praying, "Lord, help me discover the 'Peace to this house' statement for this pastor." After building trust, I would share a couple of observations with him and his supervisor along with some customized training for him. One day I was working with a young Filipino pastor who lived in the squatter areas of Manila serving the poor. I noticed he had a very natural way of asking anyone he met this simple question, "May I pray for you and your family?" He never experienced a negative response and on many occasions it led to a deep spiritual conversation. When we sat down to debrief about my visit and share my observations, I asked him, "Is it a common practice for you to ask people if you could pray for them?" His response was, "Yes, I really believe in the power of prayer and want to bless people." I followed up with another question, "Do people ever turn down your offer?" "Rarely" he replied. My response was, "I am not sure, but I think we have discovered the 'Peace to this house' statement for your cultural context." And then I proceeded to teach him Jesus' Person of Peace Principle from Luke 10:5-6. I also encouraged him to systemically go through the 400 squatter huts in his area and to approach each family by introducing himself and asking that simple question: "May I pray for you and your family?" If they respond positively follow Jesus' instructions and build a relationship with them. That young pastor built a solid church and became an excellent church planter.

So what is the conversational starter in your cultural context that will reveal if a person is spiritually receptive or not?

Do you believe people are on a spiritual journey?

As a new church pastor I prayed for eighteen months, "Lord, help me discover that 'Peace to this house' statement in my community." In the late 80's and early 90's there was a noticeable increased awareness of spirituality in our culture. The one I landed on early in my ministry adventure was, "Do you believe people are on a spiritual journey?" I didn't ask them a direct question such as, "Are you on a spiritual journey?" That would have been intrusive. But in asking them about their opinion of others they frequently revealed their personal belief and spiritual curiosity. The answer to that simple question was a great indicator of a person's spiritual receptivity. If the response was "yes" I would immediately describe to him or her what the spiritual journey looked like in relationship to Jesus.

SEARCHERS				FOLLOWERS		
Not Interested	**Curiously Seeking**	**Searching Assertively**	**Faith Commitment**	**Experiencing New Life**	**Is Growing in Community**	**Living Missionally**
• Aware but not very interested. • OK for you, but it's not for me. • Many misconceptions of Christianity. • Negative view of Christianity and religion. • Believes all religions are the same. • Has an indifferent attitude toward spiritual issues.	• Realizes there is more to life than what is seen. • Attends Christian events out of curiosity, not because of need. • Struggles with negative image of Christianity. • Questions the belief that all religions lead to the same God.	• Takes steps to find needed answers. • Intellectually believes in God. • Begins to grasp the implications of Christ's claims. • Understands the difference between Christianity and religion. • Struggles with intellectualizing Christianity.	• Realizes that they are powerless to achieve God's forgiveness. • Believes that Jesus is God and has received Him as the risen Lord and only Savior. • Has made a decision to turn their lives and wills over to the care and control of Jesus.	• Has entered into a mentoring relationship with another follower. • Grasps the meaning of the gospel and the core elements of following Jesus. • Shares Christ naturally. • Struggles with changing value system and assurance of salvation.	• Grows in intimacy with God through prayer and Bible study. • Has a deepening relationship with other followers in a local church. • Has come under the authority of Biblical values. • Experiences freedom over self-defeating habits. • Discovers not all Christians are growing.	• Craves intimacy with God through spiritual disciplines. • Shares their faith effectively. • Mentors others spiritually. • Gives generously. • Serves their community. • Understands the centrality of the gospel in their lives.
Resisting	**Questioning**	**Responding**	**Embracing**	**Adjusting**	**Stabilizing**	**Reproducing**

Using this tool that I developed over many years for these types of discussions, I would describe to listeners people who are before the cross of Christ. They are either: not interested, which is a point on the journey; curiously seeking; or assertively searching for answers to their spiritual questions. Then I would describe to them that there are people on the other side of the cross, who have picked it up and are carrying it as they follow Jesus. I would describe in simple terms the stages of one's spiritual formation. There are those who have just experienced the new life that Jesus offers, as well as those who are growing in community with other believers. Then there are those who are learning how to live missionally, by bringing Jesus into their sphere of influence and into the world. From there I would briefly describe to them the difference between those before and after the cross, which is experiencing a defining moment by embracing Jesus Christ personally as their risen Lord and only Savior.

Here are a series of four diagnostic questions that I would lead them through:

1. Where are you now on your spiritual journey?

As they read through the bullet points they begin to identify where they are on their journey. After giving them time to process through these identification markers I would gently ask them to put an X where they believe they are on their spiritual journey at this time. For some this is the first time they have ever thought of their spiritual life as a spiritual journey with significant mile markers on it.

| Not Interested | Curiously Seeking | Searching Assertively | Faith Commitment | Experiencing New Life | Is Growing in Community | Living Missionally |

2. Where would you like to be on your spiritual journey in six months to a year?

This question has its basis in a theological conviction as well as a cultural reality. Theologically, I am convinced that God is drawing people to himself (John 6:44) and culturally, I observe the fact that we live in a culture where people want to move forward or progress in their lives. So in asking the following question:

"Where would you like to be on your spiritual journey in six months to a year?" I always get a positive response along with an indication of how deeply the Spirit is moving in their lives. During this process I encourage them to put an X on that part of the journey. This is a key to understanding the depth of God's work in their lives. Their answer will reveal how the Holy Spirit is convicting them of their need for Christ. I have had people say, "I am satisfied with where I am," to people saying, "I want to be living missionally within a year."

3. What is standing between you and that point?

This question helps them discover the barriers in their lives. These barriers range from philosophical, relational, theological and personal. Here are a few examples:
- I am satisfied.
- My lack of Bible knowledge.
- My own misconceptions.
- I had a bad experience with other Christians.
- My past; God can't forgive me.

It is important here to stay positive, listen carefully and identify with the person's confusion, pain, and even remorse. This is where the breakthroughs happen and our *response* at this moment is *significant*.

If a person says, "I am satisfied," I speak to him gently and pray for him. My response is to pray for him fervently and trust God to intervene in his life.

If a person says, "I don't know anything about the Bible," I like to offer an opportunity to introduce the Bible to him through a four lesson study called Bible 101. Sometimes I will go as far as to ask if he would like to host a group of his friends to join him in the study. It is amazing to see God work in these situations. God does not work in isolation; he moves in and through our relationships and sphere of influence.

If a person responds, "My own misconceptions," I *approach him* with an opportunity to get "first-hand knowledge" through the Bible 101 study. Or, I *introduce them* to Jesus through a four week study called Christianity 101. I have discovered that nothing helps a person overcome his misconceptions like helping him personally interact with the Scriptures. Paul wrote, "Consequently, faith comes by hearing the message, and the message is heard through the word of Christ" (Romans 10:17).

If a person says, "I had a bad experience with other Christians," I *listen carefully*, empathize with his pain, and I do something that surprises him … I *apologize*. I say, "I am sorry that you had to experience that. There is no excuse for that type of behavior. All I can say is that I will seek to be a better example." This defuses the issue, builds trust and starts the healing process.

What if a person says, "My past; God can't forgive me"? In essence what he is really saying is that he cannot forgive himself. His sin is so offensive to him that he feels unworthy and unwanted by anyone. Helping him embrace the seriousness of his sin, from God's perspective, is important while exposing him to the unconditional love of God is vital. I love helping people at this point and showing them some of the forgiveness verses throughout Scripture.

4. What will it take for you to remove those barriers? Or, how can I help you take the next step?

Once you have helped a person uncover and discover some of the barriers he is facing on his spiritual journey, there will be the opportunity to assist him in taking the next steps to overcoming those barriers, by exploring and embracing the implications of Christ's claims and teachings. This is a critical moment. We must be prepared to assist people so that we do not lose the momentum of the Spirit's work. I really believe that the bulk of our evangelism training should be focused on helping people take the next steps toward the cross. Here are some common responses:

- More understanding of the Bible
- More understanding of Christianity
- Experiencing God's forgiveness
- Someone to help me
- A step of faith
- A crisis

Use this list and evaluate your personal ability to guide people into the next steps on their spiritual journey. What resources would you use? What resources are available in your church or outside your church? Remember the relational aspect of this; it will be your guide to how you walk them through the barriers they are facing.

The number one response in my experience has been "more understanding of the Bible." This is where we need to be prepared to introduce the person to the Bible, giving him an overview of the Bible and its impact, an overview of the Old and New Testaments and an introduction to Bible study methods. Bible 101 is a simple curriculum I developed to address the great need I have experienced in this area. I love seeing the expressions on people's faces when I tell them I would be willing to sit down with them for four Tuesdays and introduce them to the Bible. Most of time they look at me with great surprise and say, "You really would be willing to do that?"

Walking people through this process is like becoming a spiritual coach

Becoming a True Spiritual Coach

Walking people through this process is really like becoming a spiritual coach. You can help people through hands-on learning by asking good questions and providing practical next steps. I like to call this process "doing a spiritual assessment." All good coaches first assess the team's strengths and weaknesses along with providing an action plan for making specific progress. A spiritual assessment is discovering how deeply the Holy Spirit is at work in a person's life without alienating him/her relationally but entering into a substantive spiritual dialogue about Jesus, His life, death and resurrection and our relationship to Him. The goal is not to lead them toward a prayer of repentance but to help them embrace their barriers and develop a personalized plan for spiritual discovery or spiritual maturity.

A spiritual assessment offers the following:

- It helps identify receptivity.
- It helps uncover spiritual discovery and growth barriers.
- It helps facilitate a spiritual dialogue.
- It helps to bring focus to our spiritual discussions.
- It moves us from being spiritual salesmen seeking "to close the deal" to becoming spiritual guides.
- It provides a natural reference point for continued discussion.
- It helps provide direction for the next step.

Ways to discover the Person of Peace through using the Spiritual Journey Guide

Life Situation	Lead-in Question or Comment
Casual conversation	Do you believe people are on a spiritual journey? Can I show you something that describes what the spiritual journey looks like?
Visitation of a new family	I would like to show you a tool that reflects the vision of our church. It is our desire to help people on their spiritual journey.
Send new families in your community a welcome letter.	Our church was started on a simple concept: We help people move forward on their spiritual journey at a pace that is comfortable for them. Here is a tool called *The Journey Guide* that helps individuals discover where they are and where they want to be on their spiritual journey. This is our gift to you! If you have any questions or comments feel free to contact us.
Send out to individuals who mark, "I want	We are glad that you want to take the next step on your spiritual journey. Here is a tool called *The*

Life Situation	Lead-in Question or Comment
help in taking the next step on my spiritual journey" on the church communication card.	*Journey Guide* that helps individuals discover where they are and where they want to be on their spiritual journey. Please fill it out and a staff person will call you in the next week to set up an appointment to develop a plan for the next steps of your journey.
Newcomers class	Our church was started on a simple concept: We help people move forward on their spiritual journey at a pace that is comfortable for them. Here is a tool called *The Journey Guide* that helps individuals discover where they are on their spiritual journey.
Seeker Bible study	Before we get started in our study tonight, I want to give you this tool called *The Journey Guide.* It is designed to help you move forward on your spiritual journey. It is self-explanatory and has some easy questions for you to answer on the back. I would like you to take it home, fill it out and bring it back for next week's study. We can then help you develop a personalized plan for your spiritual journey.
Small groups	Hand out to a new member of the group: We are really glad that you have joined our small group tonight. Here is a tool we call *The Journey Guide.* It explains what our group is all about, "Helping people along their spiritual journey." After you read it, if you have any questions, I would be happy to help you through it.
Membership class	Our church was started on a simple concept: We are helping people move forward on their spiritual journey at a pace that is comfortable for them. Here is a tool called *The Journey Guide* that helps both those who are exploring Christianity and those who are growing in their faith discover where they are and where they want to be on their spiritual journey. In the Christian faith there is always another step to take in your journey with Jesus.

Life Situation	Lead-in Question or Comment
Sermon series	Several pastors have preached a seven week series on *The Journey Guide* and handed it out every Sunday. They encouraged people to fill it out and meet with a trusted friend or pastoral staff to discuss and develop a personalized plan for spiritual growth.
Vision messages	Our church was started on a simple concept: We help people move forward on their spiritual journey at a pace that is comfortable for them. Here is a tool called *The Journey Guide* that helps both those who are exploring Christianity and those who are growing in their faith discover where they are and where they want to be on their spiritual journey. In the Christian faith there is always another step to take on your journey with Jesus.

Stop, Reflect, Discuss

- How do you see this tool being used to create more focused spiritual conversations in your life?
- How could *The Spiritual Journey Guide* be used as a discipleship tool?
- How could *The Spiritual Journey Guide* be used as a way to communicate the vision of your church?

* Reproducible masters of Bible 101 & Christianity 101 can be attained through www.yourjourney.org.

Chapter 5

Creating Thirst in Your Spiritual Conversations

"You are the light of the world...let your light shine before men, that they may see your good deeds and praise your Father in heaven."
— Matthew 5:14, 16

When people are parched from the lack of liquids in their body, they naturally begin to crave for some level of relief and search for something to satisfy their thirst. This not only happens physically but I believe it happens spiritually as well. When a person is spiritually parched, they seek all sorts of ways to experience relief from their spiritual emptiness. These could range from an all-out effort to achieve success by any measure to quieting this nagging need by numbing themselves with addictive substances and unbridled pleasure-seeking.

As a pastor I engaged people from all parts of the spectrum, including the corporate executive who has enough money to meet any physical need or creature comfort his heart desires but finds out that they don't satisfy his soul. One of these gentlemen in my life described himself as "topped out" instead of "bottomed out." I have also worked with those who are bottomed out and have wrecked their lives through an array of painful addictions that ended up torturing their souls rather that relieving them. There are spiritually thirsty people all around us, from the executive who has to lay off ten thousand employees to the manager who was laid off. There is the returning vet who has tried to kill his painful memories by killing off as many brain cells as possible and the anxious college student who keeps prolonging his academic career because graduating means having to grow up.

How do you identify those thirsty souls? How do you help them discover that the pain in their heart or that unrelenting drive is really an unsatisfied spiritual need?

Learning how to create thirst in our conversations is one way to help us identify the work of God in a person's soul.

Here is a bit of wisdom to help you create thirst in your spiritual conversations:

1. Look for God's work in the lives of people

In light of man's natural bent away from God and the things of God (Ephesians 2:1-3) we can easily see the hand of God drawing in someone. Leonard Sweet said in a recent interview, "Postmodern evangelism is recognizing that God is already at work in people's lives before we arrive on the scene and that our role is helping people to see how God is present and active in their lives, calling them home." The Father is drawing people to himself (John 6:44). The Son is seeking the lost (Luke 19:10). The Holy Spirit is convicting the world (John 16:8). All we need to do is figure out how to get into God's redemptive flow and recognize his hand on the lives of those around us.

If someone expresses interest in Jesus, the Bible or church...these are good signs. If people are taking steps forward such as attending events, worship services, small groups or if someone is open to a conversation with you on spiritual things...this is God at work. We need our complete focus and our dependence to be on God because He is at work right in front of us. In reality, evangelism is more about "spotting" than creating. It is more about "joining" than even initiating.

2. Be willing to take a risk

Darryn Scheske, one of the best evangelists I know, writes, "In my experience, engaging in Spirit-led spiritual conversations with others always requires me to take a personal risk of some kind. You see, nearly every opportunity to have a spiritual conversation will produce some kind of anxiety in me. Usually I'm too tired. Or, I'm on my way somewhere else and I really don't have the time. Or, I might be intimidated by the person; their life circumstances or credentials. I might just be afraid of what they will think. If you're going to seek out spiritual conversations, they won't come when you're ready or available. They happen in the middle of your everyday life." When is the last time you put yourself out there relationally and evangelistically? This combination of excitement and anxiety is really a description of faith. I like to say that this tension in our gut is the way God calls us to exercise our faith in those situations. Whether these conversations are fruitful or not, if you act in faith, God is pleased. (Hebrews 11:6 NIV)

3. Learn to ask good questions

Being too direct can come across as intrusive and pushy. Trusting the Holy Spirit to plant and nurture the seeds that have been sown through good questions is vital to creating and sustaining spiritual conversations. Randy Newman, the author of *Questioning Evangelism,* once said, "By asking questions in our evangelism, our questions can lead to conversions, rather than presentations that lead to preconceptions. An exchange of ideas might lead both participants to the truth of the gospel. For one participant, it will be the first arrival at that point; for the other participant, it will be a rediscovery and a new appreciation of the message of the Cross."

Here are a couple questions I have used:

- Do you believe people are on a spiritual journey?
- Do you have any type of spiritual heritage in your background?
- Have you read a good book on spirituality lately?
- Have you ever heard what the difference is between Christianity and religion?
- When you think about God what image comes into your mind?

4. Get into their stories

Getting people talking about themselves is *key* to discovering God's work in their lives. The more you get them talking, the more you can see the hand of God at work in their lives. Remember, it is not about you, it is about *them* and *their* lives, *their* journey and *their* eternity. Every follower of Christ should read the classic relational text, "How to Win Friends and Influence People" by Dale Carnegie. This timeless text is based on the biblical principle: "Do to others as you would have them do to you" (Luke 6:31). Relational prowess will increase as you connect sincerely and authentically with the world around you.

5. Secure permission to go deeper

Securing permission is simply a loving and polite act to move the conversation to another level. When you ask for permission you are communicating to them that you value their privacy and time and that you are not pushing your agenda on them but seeking to serve them. Getting permission to go deeper can take a couple of different turns: 1) You could ask to explore a question or topic further; "Do you have time to explore the topic more in-depth?" 2) You could ask for their permission to tell the story around your spiritual journey; "My spiritual journey was an eye opening experience. Do you have a minute for me to give you the Cliff notes version?" 3) You could ask for their OK in offering a suggested resource or the next step in the relationship; "Could I send you an article on the subject? It might be helpful in giving you another perspective."

> Securing permission is simply a loving and polite act to move the conversation to another level

There is an old saying, "It is much easier to apologize than it is to get permission." That might work in getting your own way in business but it is a poor rule for getting into an authentic spiritual conversation. You will *never* go wrong in seeking one's permission to go deeper.

6. Guard your heart

The heart never lies! People smell a "fake" from a mile away. A genuine love for people and a servant's spirit is attractive to people. If my motives are questionable people will intuitively perceive it. We all need to take heed to Peter's words, "But in your hearts set apart Christ as Lord. Always be prepared to give an answer to everyone who asks you to give the reason for the hope that you have. But do this with gentleness and respect, keeping a clear conscience, so that those who speak maliciously against your good behavior in Christ may be ashamed of their slander" (I Peter 3:15-17). Gentleness is power under control. The gospel is described as the 'power of God' (Romans 1:16). This power needs to be handled with a gentle spirit and with great reverence for God and human destiny. Those who act forcefully and rudely lack a trust in the power of the gospel and tend to trust the manipulative techniques of man.

Stop, Reflect, And Discuss:

- What are key indicators that God is at work in your conversations?
- When was the last time you experienced a spiritual risk in a relationship?
- What are good questions that you have used to gauge a person's receptivity to spiritual things?
- What are some ways you can get people talking about themselves?
- Describe ways you actively 'guard your heart'.

Chapter 6

Tell Your Story Well

"But you will receive power when the Holy Spirit comes on you; and you will be my witnesses in Jerusalem, and in all Judea and Samaria, and to the ends of the earth."
— Acts 1:8

C hristianity has spread over the centuries through the stories of those who have had a personal encounter with the risen Lord Jesus. Every person throughout the ages whether rich, poor, powerful or obscure has a story that is precious to God. Learning to tell your faith story well is one of the best investments you can make to start and sustain your spiritual conversations. In his book, *Evangelism Out of the Box*, Rich Richardson emphasizes the importance of storytelling in our postmodern era, "Storytelling helps follow the rules of experiential truth." In other words, telling stories makes sense both emotionally and experientially to our audience. He continues, "If something rings true for us experientially and we can be authentic and non-manipulative in the way we tell the story, people will respond" (pg 93).[1] There is nothing more powerful than the fresh story of a new follower of Jesus. This is the first story you should learn to share—and you should learn to share it naturally, well and often.

Traditionally I have used a simple three-part guideline that can serve as a template in helping others write a well-told faith story:

- Before I made a faith commitment to Jesus I experienced...
- I realized I needed to trust and follow Jesus when...
- After entrusting my life to Christ, I have experienced...

But recently I came across "the before-and-after pattern" Bill Hybels writes about in his book, *Just Walk Across the Room*. He writes, "The promise of the gospel's transforming power is when you come to Christ, your old self is evicted and a new self arrives. When you tell your story, the critical contrast to draw for someone is this: What difference has Christ really made in your life? In other words, what were you like before Christ, and now what are you like after you've asked Christ to intervene?" (pg 122).[2] He continues, "It's as simple as this friends. Who were you before, and who are you now, as a result of Christ's passionate intervention in your journey?"

- I was striving...but now I'm grateful
- I was self-destructive...but now I'm healthy
- Guilty...but now liberated
- Fear-stricken...but now confident
- Despairing...but now hopeful

It's worth searching your heart and soul to firm up the three-pronged foundation of your story: The **key word or concept** that describes who you were before you met Christ; the fact that you then **came into a relationship** with Christ; and the key word or concept that describes who you are after **walking with Christ** for a time (pg 126-127).[3]

What would happen if every member, every ministry leader, and every staff person were equipped to share their before-and-after story in a compelling manner through the power of the Holy Spirit? We encourage pastors and church planters to require a written before-and-after story for church membership, for baptism candidates, and for all those desiring to participate in a child dedication ceremony. In the spiritual formation materials that I have developed, new Christians will have written their story at least three times by the time they finish their first ten lessons. Don't ignore the power of a well-told faith story!

> The essence of evangelism is simply sharing what the risen Lord Jesus has done in your life

Sharing your story not only brings light to a world in darkness but it also transforms the soul of the person sharing it. The Apostle Paul wrote to his friend Philemon, "I pray that you may be active in sharing your faith, so that you will have a full understanding of every good thing we have in Christ" (Philemon 1:6).

One week after surrendering my life to Christ I was invited by a friend to attend a seminar on evangelism that our church was sponsoring. At the time I didn't even know what the word evangelism meant but I went because several of my new friends were attending. After spending a whole day trying to figure out what was going on and being overwhelmed with techniques and tactics of evangelism, I was attending the last session of the day when the presenter said, "The essence of evangelism is simply sharing what the risen Lord Jesus has done in your life." When the day was finished my friends asked me if I wanted to go with them to the local college campus and put into practice what we learned that day. Two weeks after embracing the risen Lord Jesus as my Savior I was sharing my faith story with college students. The foundational lesson I took away from that experience was that "Jesus has given me a unique, one-of-a-kind story to tell so I should learn to tell it well and I should learn to tell it often."

Stop, Reflect, Do

- Write out your faith story using the before and after pattern.
- Share your story with three people this week.

Chapter 7
Engaging in More Spiritual Conversations

"He who wins souls is wise."
— Proverbs 11:30

A s noted earlier, evangelism has moved in the last twenty-five years from being a monologue (one-sided conversation) to a dialogue (two-way conversation). There are people all around us who are receptive to spiritual discussions and open to genuine spiritual guidance. George Barna sites that, "62% of American adults consider themselves to be not merely 'religious,' but 'deeply spiritual.'" This means that there is more than a 50-50 chance of getting into some type of spiritual conversation with people who travel in and out of your life. Learning to engage people in a meaningful, spiritual dialogue is critical for a spiritual leader.

Here are five ideas for increasing the spiritual conversations in your life:

1. Make It a Priority

It is important for missionally minded followers of Jesus to think strategically about their conversations throughout the week. If you don't plan it or make room for it, the likelihood is that it is not going to get done. I agree with the statement, "We should count conversations rather than conversions, not because I don't believe in conversions, but because I don't think we'll get many conversions if we keep emphasizing them." The number of conversations you have is directly related to the number of conversions you will see happen over a year. In coaching church leaders we use the 3 by 5 rule. If leaders are going to be serious about connecting with people, they need to uncover at least 5 new contacts a day, equaling about 35 a week, which will lead to 3 "sit-downs" for a meaningful conversation.

2. Pray for Opportunities

I remember praying one morning, "Lord, it has been awhile since I led someone to you. Open the doors and show me who I need to speak to today." As soon as I finished praying that prayer a man walked over to me and said, "Doesn't that book (my pocket Bible) get old after a while?" to which I replied, "It gets better every time I read it. Would you like to read it?" He took the Bible and began reading it. This resulted in a number of great conversations that eventually led to him and his family attending our church and embracing Jesus as Lord and Savior.

I can't remember the original source of this list but it has personally served me well as I have prayed for loved ones and friends over the years.

- That God draws them to Himself - John.6:44
- That they seek to know God - Acts 17:27
- That they believe the Scriptures - 1 Thessalonians
- That Satan is bound from blinding them to the truth - Matthew 13:19
- That the Holy Spirit works in them - John 16:8-13
- That God sends someone to lead them to Christ - Matthew 9:37, 38
- That they believe in Christ as Savior - John 5:24
- That they turn from sin - Acts 17:30-31; Acts 3:19
- That they confess Christ as Lord – Romans 10:9-10
- That they yield all to follow Christ - 2 Corinthians 5:15
- That they take root and grow in Christ - Colossians 2:6-7

3. Get out and into your community

All too often we are isolated from the world in which we live. Bill Hybels writes in his book, *Just Walk Across the Room*, "The longer a person attends church, the fewer evangelistic discussions they engage in with family members and friends. Fewer presentations of the life-changing plan of salvation are given, and fewer invitations to events that attractively present the message of Christ are offered, mostly because Christ followers have fewer friends outside the faith to whom to offer them." (pg 61)[1] Look at your calendar and see what fills your week. I encourage spiritual leaders to think about tithing their time to community service and interaction. As a leader I put in sixty plus hours a week. This means about six hours a week to be out in the community; like playing in a noon basketball league on Tuesdays and Thursdays or coaching my children's baseball and football teams. My week would be filled with serving on various community committees within the school district or through the Chamber of Commerce. It might also involve attending community events or joining professional groups such as Toastmasters International. I could easily fill up my six hours a week. Opportunities abound when we get out into our communities. A friend of mine joined a local entrepreneurial networking group. After a couple of months of being in this group, he was wondering why he was there and was feeling out of place. Then a crisis took place within the group and he discovered that he instantly become "the chaplain" of the group which led to many spiritual conversations.

> **Networking is more about joining than it is about just hanging out**

Networking is more about joining than it is about just hanging out in coffee shops, bookstores and restaurants. In a recent coaching conversation with a church planting pastor I asked him to describe his relational interactions for the week and as he was describing them to me a light went on in his head. He said, "All my interactions this week were with Christians. How do I get out of the church and into the community?" I recommended he join something such as a community service group, book club or community leadership team. He will be making a commitment not just to causes but to relationships and it will be within those relationships that God will reveal his redemptive ways.

Can you imagine all the spiritual conversations that could take place if you were to tithe your time to community service and interaction?

4. Establish routines and cultivate relationships

Beyond the tithe of your time in your community I encourage leaders to establish routines and patterns so that you build a relational presence with business owners and servers. Think strategically about all your interactions and pray that you can be a redemptive influence within that social network. A couple of telltale signs of this are, "Do people know your name?" or "Do you know people's names?" Reggie McNeal loves to ask his servers, "I am going to pray for my meal and I always pray for my server. Is there anything I can pray for you specifically?" I can see this really working as you cultivate relationships and move them from the mundane to the spiritual.

Jesus, Paul and James used the analogy of the farmer when it came to spiritual leaders patiently sowing, working and cultivating the message of the gospel. When engaging in spiritual conversations you need to have an attitude of a farmer, faithfully working and cultivating your community. The first two suggestions deal with the leader's attitude, the next two suggestions deal with putting leaders in a position for engagement. I learned a simple lesson over twenty-five years ago from an old missionary who said these words to me, "Gary, you can't serve God where you're not!" That statement helped me move away from dreaming about future ministry to engaging myself in the daily personal ministry right in front of me every day.

5. Be available to those around you

As a movement leader my life has always been on the move, traveling at a high rate of velocity and darting from one appointment or project to another, trying to catch my breath between meetings, and yet God moves according to His time frame, not mine. I have to admit that because of my busyness and people-intensive schedule that there are times that I just get "peopled out." I don't have the mental, emotional or physical energy for another spiritually intense conversation. I end up hoping that the person next to me on the plane will just keep to themselves because I am just too tired. Then after about thirty minutes into the flight God pricks my conscience and I repent and look for ways to start up a conversation to see if God will open a door in this person's life.

As pastors and leaders we need to be spiritually sensitive to those Divine opportunities where God can use us in His redemptive plan. Paul asked for prayer in this matter in his letter to the church in Ephesus: "Pray also for me, that whenever I open my mouth, words may be given me so that I will fearlessly make known the mystery of the gospel, for which I am an ambassador in chains. Pray that I may declare it fearlessly, as I should" (Ephesians 6:19-20). Remember, Paul was under house arrest and chained to a Roman soldier. Every word he spoke was under the listening ear of a potential convert. I am sure there were times when Paul was weary and just plain "peopled out." This could be behind his appeal for prayer on the matter.

There are times when we need to push beyond weariness and busyness and allow God to interrupt our agendas and schedules. I was reminded of this recently. I was running from one event to another when a young man stepped into my life after I preached at one of our new churches. I had never met him before but he said he needed to speak with me. I stopped for a moment, listened to his story and saw in his eyes that this was his time…his day of redemption…his moment to embrace Jesus as Lord and Savior. An hour later this confused young man was a new man in Christ. I was a part of God's redemptive plan because I was spiritually sensitive and willing to let my schedule be interrupted. After that experience God's Spirit pricked my heart with this thought, "How many times have I missed those Divine opportunities because I have been unavailable or insensitive?"

Stop, Reflect, Discuss

- How many contacts does it take for you to get a meaningful sit-down with a person?
- When is the last time you asked God to open new doors of opportunity for you?
- If you were to tithe your time to community service and interaction what would your work week look like?
- What relational commitments are you making in your community?
- What places do you frequent in your community?
- How do you overcome spiritual insensitivity created by your weariness and busyness?

Chapter 8

Six Causes for Evangelistic Entropy

"Consecrate yourselves, for tomorrow the LORD will do amazing things among you."
– Joshua 3:5

Entropy is the natural and irreversible tendency toward disorder in any system without an external source of energy (The Wordsmyth English Dictionary).[1] When we apply this principle to evangelism we need to embrace the fact that left to itself the energy for evangelism in the local church will naturally (and in some cases irreversibly) move toward disorder. This is why every church needs an energy source to counter this natural drift from mission to maintenance. What is that energy source? Leadership! It's through leaders who model evangelistic passion, through their prayers, priorities and plans. Someone once said, "Leadership is focused energy bursts." The older the church, the more energy is needed to overcome all the competing issues that cause evangelistic entropy. In this chapter we are going to take a close look at how to practically lead your church to overcome the entropy that can slowly kill a church's missional effectiveness.

Here are the six causes for evangelistic entropy:

1. Burnout of the Leader

Evangelism is a spiritually intense activity. Pioneer church planters, those without a "running start" with a core group, are fully engaged in evangelistic activities out of the sheer need for survival. The ability to network in the community and to engage it evangelistically rests solely on their shoulders, and the burden of that responsibility is intense. The constant load of rejection they encounter can lead to burnout. One young leader said to me, "If you really want to gain a little understanding on the condition of the church in America just drop yourself into a community not knowing a soul. Every time I shared my vision with churched people they looked at me as though I was an alien from another planet." The face of that constant rejection can be very demoralizing.

Another factor that can lead to burnout is the lonely nature of the job, especially for those who come out of thriving ministries. The shock of going to a community where nobody really cares that you are there can be debilitating. I usually try to prepare pioneer church planters with a little pep talk like, "When you move into town you will need to push yourself to meet people because the only people who care that you are there will be me and Jesus!" Now that is an overstatement. I am sure that there are many people who care that they are there. The only problem is that none of them live in that town. Leadership is a lonely job! Many pastors feel like they are carrying the burden for their communities alone. Listening to people's myriad of complaints can lead to frustration and wondering if anyone cares about their neighbors.

The final factor that can lead to burnout is the intense care of new believers. Converts come in all sizes and shapes, with all sorts of baggage. They have messed-up marriages, damaged emotional lives, self-centered values, screwed-up finances and whacked-out priorities. They have no knowledge of God, the Bible and the church. Seeing them through these issues with proper follow-up and discipleship can be a very draining and frustrating experience. I particularly remember one such time when I cried out to God. It was eighteen months after we had started a new church. I was working a couple of jobs. We had grown from two families to about 40 families, of which about 80-90% were people who weren't believers yet, had just trusted Christ, or had just started coming back to Christ. I remember yelling at God saying, "If you don't bring me any help in the next six months…I am going to quit!" Did it mean that I didn't love lost people? No! It just revealed that I was burned out. John Maxwell has said, "There's no such thing as burnout. It's just people who are taking themselves too seriously." In principle I believe that. But when you're on the frontlines and ministry is such a struggle, you seriously do need some tangible help. The end of that story is that within two weeks God provided two spiritually mature couples who partnered with us in establishing the church!

2. Imbalance of Ministry Priorities

Imbalance is another reason why leaders can abdicate their evangelistic responsibilities. Although many churches mission statements say something about reaching *unchurched* people, the truth is that investing in *churched* people takes time. A leader's time can get swallowed up just ministering to the already convinced. Shepherding, counseling, discipling, and training all take time; not including leading and preparing for worship services. If leaders are not disciplined in networking and spending time with unchurched people they can end up growing a church for the churched instead of a leading the church to missionally engage its community. We recommend that our pastors and church planters minimally tithe of their work week in networking and developing pre-Christian contacts. To adequately address evangelism entropy leaders are going to have to replace a negative imbalance with a positive imbalance in favor of evangelistic engagement and equipping the church missionally.

There is a concept out there called "corporate entropy" which is simply defined as energy waste. Energy waste occurs through such things as the endless red tape of organizations, team inefficiency and the surrendering to constant distractions. It is simply "energy lost to waste," such as waste of time, money and human resources. If corporate entropy is not recognized and addressed by leaders it will bring on inertia, complacency, denial, missed opportunities, vulnerability to paradigm shifts, competitive attacks and permanent loss of vitality. Does this describe your church or organization when it comes to outreach?

3. "Sin in the Camp"

Have you ever wondered why some churches and organizations strangely lose their evangelistic edge and effectiveness? After being involved in denominational ministry for over 12 years, I have discovered that the spiritual principle from Joshua 6-7 is applicable today. Unfortunately, there is a dark side of the church that is rarely seen except by those who are in charge of its care and oversight. In my limited experience I have seen churches derailed by sexual misconduct, financial scandals and timid leadership. There are leaders who are fearful to confront sin, to take a hard look at themselves and to make the needed changes to keep the church on mission.

Yet all too often these hidden and debilitating sins go undetected because leaders don't recognize or embrace this principle. In Joshua 6 we see God's people on the move, fully engaged in the mission that God had charged them with; securing the Promised Land. In the midst of that great victory, one of the victorious violated God's specific command (Josh. 6:18). The result of that sin was the only reason they experienced a humiliating defeat over a weaker enemy. Jericho, a city of over a million people, was conquered by a small band of believers trusting in the hand of God and, Ai, a city of 12,000, defeated the people of God because of one man's selfish act and rebellion against a Holy God. This reminds us that a spiritual mission is only completed by spiritual means. Read God's response to Joshua's lament in Joshua 7:10-12:

> "The LORD said to Joshua, 'Stand up! What are you doing down on your face? Israel has sinned; they have violated my covenant, which I commanded them to keep. They have taken some of the devoted things; they have stolen, they have lied, they have put them with their own possessions. That is why the Israelites cannot stand against their enemies; they turn their backs and run because they have been made liable to destruction. I will not be with you anymore unless you destroy whatever among you is devoted to destruction.'"

Not a lot of sympathy here. Pretty simple message: Get up, deal with it and move on! The LORD continues and instructs Joshua on how to deal with it, "Go, consecrate the people. Tell them, 'Consecrate yourselves in preparation for tomorrow; for this is what the LORD, the God of Israel, says: That which is devoted is among you, O Israel. You cannot stand against your enemies until you remove it.'" (Josh. 7:13)

I liken "consecration" to doing a rigorous spiritual inventory. As individuals there are seasons in our lives where we need to allow Scripture to search our hearts and penetrate our lives. Martin Luther made it a regular practice to pray through the 'Ten Commandments' and 'The Fruit of the Spirit' asking God to expose those hidden areas that made him spiritually weak.

How does one lead a church to consecrate themselves? Here are a couple of "quick hits" to ponder:

- Make personal consecration a regular practice in the life of your people. Ask individuals to assess their spiritual life through a rigorous spiritual inventory. When was the last time you taught on the subject within your congregation? Example: Pray through I Corinthians 13.
- Make corporate consecration a regular practice. As a leadership team submit yourselves to internal and external assessments. What type of internal and external assessments has your church participated in? Example: Pray through Revelation 2 and 3 as a leadership team.
- Restore the act of corporate confession. Agreeing with God corporately that as a church we are stuck, complacent, crippled by disunity, etc. When is the last time you led your congregation in a time of public confession?
- Promoting prayers of resolution or commitment. Lead your church through defining moments of commitment to glorify God and to

missional engagement. Can you remember the last time you asked your congregation to drive a "stake in the ground" symbolizing their commitment? Read Joshua 24 to glean some principles on leading your church through a time of resolution and commitment.

Do you feel like there is something strangely crippling your evangelistic effectiveness? Are there times where you sense that something beyond you is holding you back? Ask God to search you and your church. Courageously ask God to reveal the source of your trouble.

4. Unwilling to Pay the Price

What price are you willing to pay to see your church actively engaged in evangelism? Price? What do I mean by price? There is a cost for everything. One of the causes for evangelistic entropy is an unwillingness to count the cost of growth. If evangelism is really going to be a value that your church embraces, the church will have to embrace the changes that will take place when evangelism is activated in the church. The following questions will help you measure your readiness to count the cost:

- What leadership changes are you unwilling to sacrifice? Too many times leaders get locked in and set in their ways which leads to becoming self-protective. Once a self-protective posture grabs the heart of any leader every decision or action is filtered through this question: How is this going to impact me?
- What programs are you unwilling to touch? Do you have a way to assess the effectiveness of your programs? Are there programs in place that exist only because of tradition and not in light of their added value to the mission?
- What is the bottom line you are willing to spend? How much of your budget is allocated for evangelism? Five, ten, twenty, forty percent? Is there a price too high to pay?
- What relationships are you unwilling to let go? What if your best friend strongly opposed you? What if long-term relationships became threatened in light of decisions that needed to be made?
- What types of environmental changes are you unwilling to make? What about stylistic changes in your services? What about social-economic changes in the nature of your congregation? What about the look and feel of your facilities?
- What personal price is too high? What financial, emotional, relational, physical costs are too heavy to bear?

Let the words of Jesus wash over your soul from Luke 9:57-62: "As they were walking along the road, a man said to him, 'I will follow you wherever you go.' Jesus replied, 'Foxes have holes and birds of the air have nests, but the Son of Man has no place to lay his head.' He said to another man, 'Follow me.' But the man replied, 'Lord, first let me go and bury my father.' Jesus said to him, 'Let the dead bury their own dead, but you go and proclaim the kingdom of God.' Still another said, 'I will follow you, Lord; but first let me go back and say good-bye to my family.' Jesus replied, 'No one who puts his hand to the plow and looks back is fit for service in the kingdom of God.'"

There IS cost involved with being in the center of God's missional purpose. If we are going to bring leadership energy to the evangelistic entropy that you are facing, the cost will be real. Dwight Eisenhower said, "There is no victory at bargain basement prices."

5. Tyranny of the Urgent

The fifth cause of evangelistic entropy is what is known as the "tyranny of the urgent." I discovered this concept in Stephen Covey's classic book, *Seven Habits of Highly Effective People*. In it he refers to two factors that determine activity: urgency and importance.

Urgent items are described as "...those that are requiring immediate attention. It's 'Now!' Urgent things act on us...urgent matters are usually visible. They press on us. They insist on action. They're often popular with others. They are usually right in front of us. And often they are pleasant, easy, and fun to do. But so often unimportant!"

Important items are described as "...being focused on results. If something is important, it contributes to your mission, your values, and your high priority goals. Important matters that are not urgent require more initiative."

Let's consider the four quadrants of Covey's urgent/important matrix as it relates to all the activities that rob us and our churches of evangelistic energy. Take a few minutes to categorize your daily and weekly activities in the following quadrants.

Here are some "what, who and when" questions to consider as you work through the urgent/important matrix:

What

- What are the important activities that you cannot delegate?
- What are the important activities that you can delegate?
- What are the not important activities that you cannot delegate?
- What are the not important activities that you can delegate?

Who

- Who assists you in navigating the not important activities of your day?
- Who can help you in completing the important/urgent activities of your day?
- Who assists you in scheduling time for the important/non-urgent activities of your day?
- Who can you trust with the important/urgent activities in your ministry?

When

- When in your weekly schedule is there time for important/urgent activities?
- When in your weekly schedule is there time for important/non-urgent activities?
- When in your annual calendar is there time for reflecting and planning important/urgent activities?
- When in your annual calendar is there time for reflecting and planning important/non-urgent activities?

As stated earlier, leadership is simply a well applied burst of energy. If a leader is going to let his energy get depleted through not important and urgent activities that distract every ministry, then there will not be any energy left to counteract the evangelistic entropy that attacks every church and robs it of its evangelistic effectiveness.

6. Ineffective Training Strategy

Recently I discovered an athletic training principle called momentary muscular failure, also known as the overload principle. This principle states that, "Only by stressing your muscles beyond their physical capacity can you compel them to produce an adaptive response and exact a change in your body. You will gradually increase intensity until you are training to momentary muscular failure. From a training perspective, failure equals success! When you first attempt to train to failure, it can be an enlightening experience, one that you might not be prepared to endure. While lifting a weight, most people are prone to give up mentally before their muscles truly give out. They may think they have induced muscular failure, yet their muscles are capable of completing several more repetitions. To obtain the best results, you must learn to differentiate between mental failure and physical failure. Remember the adage, 'What doesn't kill you makes you stronger?' Pushing yourself to the limit will show your internal and external strength and allow your body to achieve more than you ever could have imagined." (Human Kinetics)

The take away of this principle is that for effective training to take place, participants must experience a certain level of discomfort. They must be pushed out of their comfort zone. Which begs the question: "How much of our training pushes people out of their comfort zones?" or "How much of our training is simply entertainment for the consumer?" Jesus in His Great Commission says, ...and teach them to obey everything I have commanded." (Matthew 28:20) Obedience is a bending of our wills to another's will. A disciple of Jesus is one who bends his will to the commands of Jesus. In a day when megachurches are admittedly saying we don't know how to make disciples, this principle goes to the heart of the matter.

Here are five biblical elements needed for an effective training strategy:

1. A Mature Influence:
  Jesus said, "A student is not above his teacher, but everyone who is fully trained will be like his teacher" (Luke 6:40). Paul writes that fathers are to train their children (Ephesians 6:4) and the older women are to train younger women (Titus 2:3-4). I am personally convinced that the goal of every church should be that all converts have a personal mentor, a mature influence that builds trust, sets the example and speaks specifically into their lives as they bend their will to Jesus' will.

2. A Common Goal:
  Paul wrote to a young leader he was mentoring, "Have nothing to do with godless myths and old wives' tales; rather, train yourself to be godly. For physical training is of some value, but godliness has value for all things, holding promise for both the present life and the life to come" (I Timothy 4:7-8). Godliness is defined as, "character and conduct determined by the principle of love or fear of God in the heart." Another definition describes godliness as "a God-ward attitude, does that which is well-pleasing to Him." If the goal is to please ourselves or meet our own needs then every effort of training will always fall short.

3. A Common Source of Authority:

Jesus said, "and teach them to obey everything I have commanded" (Matthew 28:20). Paul wrote, "All Scripture is God-breathed and is useful for teaching, rebuking, correcting and training in righteousness, so that the man of God may be thoroughly equipped for every good work" (II Timothy 3:16-17). Following the rules is essential to training, yet so often we all want to write our own rules or live by our interpretation of the rules and then we wonder why our efforts are so ineffective!

4. A Certain Level of Discomfort:

Paul uniquely describes the training process when he writes, "All Scripture is God-breathed and is useful for teaching, rebuking, correcting and training in righteousness, so that the man of God may be thoroughly equipped for every good work" (II Timothy 3:16-17). Teaching is giving us the knowledge needed to be thoroughly equipped. Rebuking is revealing behavior, attitudes and beliefs that keep us from being thoroughly equipped. Correcting involves those mid-course adjustments that are needed to be thoroughly equipped. Training in righteousness is the discipline needed to stay the course and achieve the goal of godliness. In the book of Hebrews we see the value of discipline, "No discipline seems pleasant at the time, but painful. Later on, however, it produces a harvest of righteousness and peace for those who have been trained by it" (Hebrews 12:11).

5. Constant Repetition:

I think all of us would agree that the more we do something the better equipped we feel at handling a certain task. The author of the book of Hebrews writes, "But solid food is for the mature, who by constant use have trained themselves to distinguish good from evil" (Hebrews 5:14). What level of repetition is represented in your training programs?

As previously stated, leadership is "energy bursts." If we are going to combat evangelistic entropy we are going to need to bring a strategically aimed energy burst to our evangelistic efforts. I have had the privilege of coaching individuals in the area of personal evangelism and helping spiritual leaders increase the number of spiritual conversations they get into in a normal week. The biggest thing that happens in these coaching relationships is that leaders get focused! They focus on God and His work in their world which leads them to opportunities they have never seen before. One young pastor after I had coached him engaged in more spiritual conversations in three months than he had in his previous four years of ministry.

Stop, Reflect, Discuss:

- How does burnout affect your ability to engage in meaningful outreach?
- How much time in a week do you spend in meaningful relationships with those outside the church?
- Have you ever done a rigorous spiritual inventory of your life?
- How much of your time is eaten up with non-outreach activities?
- How are the five elements of training being lived out in your church's evangelism and discipleship plan?

Chapter 9

Sharpening Your Evangelistic Skills

"If the ax is dull and its edge unsharpened,
more strength is needed but skill will bring success."
— Ecclesiastes 10:10

L eaders are passionate learners. Leaders are always seeking ways to improve themselves by sharpening their skills. They fully embrace the fact that growing leaders lead growing organizations. If you are going to sharpen the edge of your personal evangelism skills, it is going to take courage, imagination and discipline. There is always a price to be paid for growth. The cost will involve significant amounts of time, energy and resources, along with a significant level of vulnerability, which says, "I am not as effective as I could be and I need help to get better." Here are five ways to sharpen your evangelistic skills:

1. Read a good book on evangelism

Every year as part of my own leadership development I read a book on evangelism. This year I am reading *Permission Evangelism* by Michael Simpson. This is a must read for all Christ followers who are serious about sharpening their evangelistic skills. Here is a list of the books I've read over the last several years:

- *Permission Evangelism: When to Talk When to Walk*, Michael L. Simpson
- *Question Evangelism: Engaging People's Hearts the Way Jesus Did*, Randy Newman
- *Just Walk Across The Room: Simple Steps Pointing People To Faith*, Bill Hybels

- *Outflow: Outward-focused Living in a Self-focused World*, Steve Sjogren and Dave Ping
- *More Ready Than You Realize*, Brian D. McLaren
- *Evangelism Outside the Box*, Rick Richardson
- *Building a Contagious Church*, Mark Mittelberg
- *Evangelism That Works*, George Barna
- *How To Reach Secular People*, George Hunter III
- *To Spread The Power*, George Hunter III
- *Knocking On Doors, Opening Hearts*, Ralph Neighbour

2. Find out where effective evangelism is happening and learn from those who are doing it

Recently I purchased Nelson Searcy's *Evangelism Seminar Resource*. It is filled with many ideas and practical tips for developing a comprehensive evangelism system in your local church. In the past I've ordered materials from Steve Sjogren's *Servant Evangelism* site (www.servantevangelism.com), along with subscribing to his online newsletter called 'Serve.'

3. Hang out with leaders who are doing it better than you

Some evangelistic leaders I learned from in my early days of ministry were Paul and Steve Johnson along with Tom Nebel, who is the "Master of the Evangelistic Invitation." Most recently I have learned from planters that I have coached. Darryn Scheske and Joe Basile inspire me in how they are always looking for opportunities to engage in spiritual conversation.

4. Hire an evangelistic coach

World class athletes have several coaches in their corner, watching, listening and advising them in how to improve their performance. Pastors need all types of coaches throughout the life of their ministry, such as: *Leadership coaches* to help them navigate critical leadership issues such as processing change, adding staff, creating and developing systems and *Stewardship coaches* to help them raise resources in a way that does not harm the church but builds and strengthens the church around a united vision. Communication coaches to help them take their communication skills to a new level. Many pastors themselves admit that they have struggled for years in personal evangelism. An evangelism coach will develop strategies to help pastors become more competent in sharing their faith: 1) By helping them discover their evangelistic style, 2) By assisting them in seeing the opportunities all around them, 3) By teaching them to be competent in using a reproducible tool, 4) By teaching them how to develop a clear, concise and compelling faith story, 5) By teaching them how to develop and maintain spiritual dialogues, 6) By teaching them how to develop the appropriate next steps with those they are pointing to Jesus, 7) By holding them accountable to their personal evangelistic goals, and 8) By helping them to debrief and analyze their spiritual conversations on a weekly basis. Evangelism coaches can have a dramatic impact on a pastor. Kirt Wiggins, of Pathway Community Church in Elmhurst, IL, said, "It was recommended to me to find a personal evangelism coach to help me sharpen my skills in this area. In just five months my coach helped me discover ways to share my faith each week. During that time I have had more opportunities for spiritual conversations and to see people come to Christ than ever before."

5. Just do it!

Solomon wrote "...he who wins souls is wise." (Proverbs 11:30) I always read this verse and thought, "Yeah, it is wise to win souls, pretty basic" but in reality its meaning is much deeper, "You get wisdom in the process of winning souls." It's been said, "90% of what you learn comes through actually doing whatever you are trying to learn." The more spiritual conversations that you engage in, the more wisdom you will gain in the process and the more skillful you will become in the art of spiritual dialogue. If you are not active you will have a slower learning curve. Do whatever you can to engage in meaningful spiritual conversations throughout the week.

Solomon wrote, "If the ax is dull and its edge unsharpened, more strength is needed but skill will bring success" (Ecclesiastes 10:10 NIV). Let's start sharpening our evangelistic edges this week so that we can get into the middle of God's redemptive flow.

Stop, Reflect, Discuss

- What books have you read lately on this subject?
- What seminars, websites, blogs or conferences would you recommend?
- Would you spend the time and the resources to get into a coaching relationship?
- How many spiritual conversations do you get into each week?
- Who are the leaders in your life that are doing it better than you?

Chapter 10

Increasing Your Passion

"I pray that you may be active in sharing your faith, so that you will have
a full understanding of every good thing we have in Christ."
— Philemon 6

ave you heard the old adage of, "Speed of the leader, speed of the team"?
The evangelistic temperature of any church can be measured by one
group – the spiritual leaders. If the spiritual leaders have hearts that are
broken and continue to be broken for the lost in their community it will spread
like a virus throughout the church. It will guide every decision. It will affect
their calendar. It will impact their schedules. It will be reflected in their budget.
The following are a few thoughts to help spiritual leaders raise the evangelistic
temperature of their hearts, thus raising the evangelistic temperature of their
churches.

Walk Slowly and Prayerfully through Your City

While Paul was waiting for his traveling companions in Athens he walked
through the city and his heart became 'distressed' (Acts 17:16 NIV) by what he
was seeing. His heart was broken for the wandering souls who were striving to
connect with God. It is very easy as a pastor to let our hearts become hardened
towards people. We can become hard out of our own weariness from ministry
and our frustration in leading people who don't want to be led. This is when we
need a fresh vision and a new burden for the masses of humanity right at our own
doorstep who are striving to find a connection with God. Jesus' missional heart
was broken for his people when he cried out, "O Jerusalem, Jerusalem, you who
kill the prophets and stone those sent to you, how often I have longed to gather
your children together, as a hen gathers her chicks under her wings, but you were
not willing" (Matthew 23:37 NIV). So our hearts must be broken for our cities,
our counties, our states, our country and our world.

Routinely as a pastor, I prayer walked through the heart of our city, praying for business and community leaders. During those times God would strangely warm my heart to the needs of our community as I would start to see our community through Jesus' eyes and with Jesus' heart. Is prayer walking a discipline you practice?

My friend, Dan Maxton, provides a great summary of the basics involved in prayer walking taken from *Prayer Walking*: Hawthorne and Kendrick.

Go in Teams of Three: Experience has shown that triplets work the best. Prayer walking needs to be seen as a team activity because intercessory prayer is fortified when believers agree. As teams pray together one person's wisdom reinforces another person's vision, resulting in solid, confident praying.

Use Maps: Designating areas through distributed maps can help a great deal but they are not meant to replace the Holy Spirit's guidance. Allow God to escort you to divinely appointed places and appointments. There is no limit to the creative ways to cover an area with prayer. It is good to keep a record of where and when you have prayed to identify areas of high receptivity and resistance.

Pick Specific Topics of Prayer: It is often good to fortify prayer with information. The right background data can help your team. One simple maxim that can bring balance: "Make sure God is addressed and people are blessed."

Open your Eyes: Most prayer walking is vision, which is described as "the art of seeing what you are looking at." A practical way to use "the eyes of your heart" (Ephesians 1:18) is to ask God to help you see the city with His eyes.

Pray Aloud: Prayer is not telepathy. God certainly knows what you are thinking, but Satan and the demonic hoard cannot read your mind. We must verbally call forth the power of God against the darkness that has set itself against God's purposes and people. Praying aloud does not mean praying loudly. Be respectful and do not draw negative attention to yourselves.

Pray with Scripture: Sometimes in prayer walking you see obvious needs but fail to know how to pray. Take along a small Bible when you walk.

You can turn many verses or phrases into a prayer. You can be confident of praying the Will of God when you pray the Word of God.

Pray with Relevance: Pray with sensitivity to the people and places you are actually encountering. Pray by name for those you know or meet. Pray with empathy for the families or children you might encounter. Pray for insight for the homes, shops and schools. Ask God what His will is for them.

Pray with Spiritual Warfare in Mind: You are in a battle as you start a church in a community and/or region. Some areas have strongholds that take longer to go down. Put on your spiritual armor. (See Ephesians 6)

Do You Dream of Them?

I came across a stirring quote from David Brainerd that struck a cord in my heart. "I care not where I go, or how I live, or what I endure so that I may save souls. When I sleep I dream of them; when I awake they are first in my thoughts...no amount of scholastic attainment, of able and profound exposition of brilliant and stirring eloquence can atone for the absence of a deep impassioned sympathetic love for human souls."

Brainerd's words reminded me of Paul's passionate confession in Romans 9:1-5:

> "I speak the truth in Christ—I am not lying, my conscience confirms it in the Holy Spirit—I have great sorrow and unceasing anguish in my heart. For I could wish that I myself were cursed and cut off from Christ for the sake of my brothers, those of my own race, the people of Israel. Theirs is the adoption as sons; theirs the divine glory, the covenants, the receiving of the law, the temple worship and the promises. Theirs are the patriarchs, and from them is traced the human ancestry of Christ, who is God over all, forever praised!"

A couple of recent events fired up my passion for human souls:

First, at the church where I have been preaching since Easter we had a baptismal service. Hearing men, women and children declare their personal faith in Jesus and out of obedience follow in His footsteps with the act of baptism, just stirred my heart.

Second, to celebrate Father's Day we had a family gathering with my father and my siblings. Twenty-nine years ago I experienced the miracle of God's saving grace when I got down on my knees, cried out to God and embraced Christ as my risen Lord and only Savior. Twenty-nine years ago most of my family was far from God, but as we sat around the table this Father's Day, every one of them now has their own story of faith, their own story of how God's amazing grace has invaded their hearts. My heart was filled with joy and a renewed passion that the next generation of our family be reached, touched and transformed by God's saving grace. That's my new dream! That's my first thought of the day!

Developing a Sowing Mentality

Why is it that some missional leaders see growth in their church every year? Why is it the some can crash through growth barrier after growth barrier? There are multiple issues around this subject but one thing rings true in every leader I know who hasn't settled on a plateau. Each of these leaders possesses what I like to call a 'sowing mentality.' They are constantly and liberally sowing seeds to uncover receptive hearts to the gospel. These leaders do whatever it takes to discover those who possess that 'good soil' Jesus spoke about which will produce a yield of one hundredfold.

King Solomon offers some wisdom on the subject of sowing in the book of Ecclesiastes, "*Sow your seed in the morning and at evening let not your hands be idle, for you do not know which will succeed, whether this or that, or whether both will do equally well*" (Ecclesiastes 11:6). This verse speaks volumes to those who are serious about making connections with those who are disconnected from your people and know nothing about your church.

1. Those with a 'sowing mentality' know it is a twenty-four hour job, "*Sow your seed in the morning and at evening let not your hands be idle...*"

> Sowing is a 'morning and evening' job. Missional leaders understand that God's redemptive flow is never turned off. As one leader put it, "leaders understand that the opportunity monitor is never off." Missional leaders realize that opportunities abound all around them all the time and frequently when it isn't convenient. I have become a fan of the television show "24" in recent days. I am always amazed what Jack Bauer can accomplish in a twenty-four hour period!
>
> Can you think of a DAY that changed the life of your church? That day for me was July 17, 1991. It happened after two and a half years of sowing seeds into the community and we had planned and prepared for a Friend's Day in the middle of the summer. At the beginning of the summer we were averaging sixty-five people; by the fall we were averaging 165. We saw

more people cross the line of faith that year than in the previous two years; a year later we broke the two-hundred barrier. We reaped a harvest through constantly and creatively sowing seeds into our community.

2. Those with a 'sowing mentality' know that it involves hard work, "...*let not your hands be idle...*"

Missional leadership is not for the faint of heart. It is for those who are willing to roll up their sleeves and push themselves out in the harvest field. It is for those who resist idleness. One thing I am grateful for in my childhood is that my father, who was raised on a farm, imparted to me a farmer's mentality towards work. Farming is a 24/7 job. Idleness is not in the vocabulary of a farmer nor in that of successful church planters. I heard Darrin Patrick say at a recent church planting conference that many young church planters enter church planting out of a sense of laziness because they are tired of a senior leader holding them accountable for their performance and results. These are the guys who start churches that never grow over sixty-five in total attendance.

At first I was taken back by that observation, but as a coach, I see too many young leaders and those new to full-time ministry struggle with the issue of time management and putting in a hard day's work. Time gets wasted and squandered resulting in lost opportunities. The lack of diligence in planning, preparing and cultivating your community is one of the keys to ineffective outreach. The old writer Sam Ewig said it best, "Hard work spotlights the character of people: some turn up their sleeves, some turn up their noses, and some don't turn up at all."

3. Those with a 'sowing mentality' embrace the mysterious work of God, "...*for you do not know which will succeed...*"

There is a sense of mystery to the work of God. In the parable of the sower, you get the idea from Jesus that the sower was really concerned with scattering the seed and not so much with where the seed landed. He trusted God for the fruit. His job was to get the seed out and to get it out liberally no matter what it cost. I remember our first Easter Service at our church plant. We had $1050.00 in the bank and spent $1000.00 of it on an Easter mailer of 5000 postcards. The result of this mailer was we had our highest attendance, cultivated very receptive contacts who became converts, along with attracting some significant families who became ministry partners. I remember thinking that that $1000.00 would not have made any difference if I just kept it in the bank.

Sowing seeds in faith and prayerfully trusting God to work miraculously through your efforts is essential. Scattering seed without watering with faith, fertilizing with prayer and cultivating with hard work will be like casting seed to the wind... fruitless.

4. Those with a 'sowing mentality' are not particular about methods, "...*whether this or that, or whether both will do equally well...*"

In my experience too many church leaders get stuck or inebriated with a particular style of evangelism. Yet leaders with a sowing mentality understand it is never an 'either/or' proposition but more of a 'both/ and' conviction. Equipping your people through a highly relational and incarnational style of evangelism is the first place to start but it does not rule out doing a systematic visitation or follow-up process that is built on the connections with public worship service. Equipping your people to be includers and inviters does not nullify the use of social networking, various types of marketing and branding your vision and image throughout your city. The old revivalist Leonard Ravenhill said, "Any method of evangelism will work if God is in it."

Developing a sowing mentality is a life or death proposition for any church. For a new church, if you are not sowing evangelistic seeds in your community you will die a quick death filled with inexcusable excuses. For an older church, it will be a slow and painful death built on harmful rationalizations. Both are equally tragic and embarrassing to the Lord of the Harvest. Are you reaping what you have sown?

Stop, Reflect, Discuss

- What fires up your heart when it comes to God's evangelistic purposes?
- Have you ever participated in a prayer walk?
- Discuss the following in relationship to evangelism – "those who sow sparingly will also reap sparingly."
- What are five ways you can begin to sow evangelistic seeds in your relationships and throughout your community?

Eleven Ways to Pray for Your Friends

I can't remember the original source of this list but it has personally served me well as I have prayed for loved ones and friends over the years.

1. That God draws them to Himself.
   John 6:44: "No one can come to me unless the Father who sent me draws him…"

2. That they seek to know God.
   Acts 17:27: "God did this so that men would seek Him and perhaps reach out for Him and find Him, though He is not far from each one of us."

3. That they believe the Scriptures.
   1 Thess. 2:13: "And we also thank God continually because when you received the word of God which you heard from us, you accepted it not as the word of men, but as it actually is, the word of God…"

4. That Satan is bound from blinding them to the truth.
   Matthew 13:19: "When anyone hears the message about the kingdom and does not understand it, the evil one comes and snatches away what was sown in his heart."

5. That the Holy Spirit works in them.
   John 16:8-13: "When the Holy Spirit comes, he will convict the world of guilt in regard to sin and righteousness and judgment…He will guide you into all truth…"

6. That God sends someone to lead them to Christ.
   Matthew 9:37-38: "Then he said to his disciples, 'The harvest is plentiful but the workers are few. Ask the Lord of the harvest, therefore, to send out workers into His harvest field.'"

7. That they believe in Christ as Savior.
   John 5:24: "I tell you the truth, whoever hears my word and believes him who sent me has eternal life and will not be condemned; he has crossed over from death to life."

8. That they turn from sin.
   Acts 17:30-31: "God commands all people everywhere to repent."
   Acts 3:19: "Repent, then, and turn to God, so that your sins may be wiped out, that times of refreshing may come from the Lord."

9. That they confess Christ as Lord.
   Romans 10:9-10: "if you confess with your mouth 'Jesus is Lord', and believe in your heart that God raised him from the dead, you will be saved."

10. That they yield all to follow Christ.
    2 Cor. 5:15: "And he died for all, that those who live should no longer live for themselves but for him who died for them and was raised again."

11. That they take root and grow in Christ.
    Col. 2:6-7: "So then, just as you received Christ Jesus as Lord, continue to live in him, rooted and built up in him, strengthened in the faith as you were taught, and overflowing with thankfulness."

The 3 x 5 Rule for Pastors and Missionaries

The 3 by 5 rule is simple: A leader seeks to find 5 contacts a day or 35 a week until they get 3 meetings or sit-downs to either share the gospel or the vision of the church. A contact is securing a person's name and contact information (a business card, phone number or email.) A sit-down is a follow-up appointment with one of the contacts you have generated.

The primary question generated by this rule is, "How do you find 35 contacts a week?" There are three sources of contacts we will look at today. 1) Follow-up Contacts 2) Networking Contacts and 3) Cold Calling Contacts. Here are a number of ideas around each of these sources:

Follow-up Contacts

Your Church Mailing List - If your church has any age to it, it should have a list of everyone who has come in contact with the church. This list can be generated through your worship services, special events, children's events and small groups. One thing every good church planter does is collect contact information. Farming your list to look for opportunities to have a sit-down with people is a good place to start; there is some level of receptivity here already along with a connection to build on. A number of years ago I coached a church planter to simply work the list of people he generated in a two year old church. Over the following sixty days he saw thirty people come to Christ! There are opportunities right in front of us that we never take.

Nowadays, I would use the church phone to make these calls because of the caller ID feature people have on their phones. They will probably recognize the church name more easily than an individual's name. Typically the best time to call is between 6:30 to 8:30 p.m. In the early days of our church plant I made between 25-50 calls every Monday night, usually with a 50% pick up rate. Within the call you'll want to offer them friendliness, spiritual assistance and an opportunity to meet them personally by setting up an appointment.

As our church list expanded I recruited and trained volunteers to call through the list every three to six months.

How many names do you have in your church database? When is the last time you made any personal contact with them?

Networking Contacts

Sponsoring Churches' Mailing Lists - Sit down with your sponsoring churches and their database. Look for anyone who visited their church from your area. Communicate with those pastors that you are only looking for fringe people and not key leaders. You will be amazed at how many contacts this can generate.

Local Chamber of Commerce or Local Club Member Lists - Make a courtesy contact, hear their story, learn their business and share your story of starting this new church.

Referrals – As a church planter, I never had a conversation without asking this question: Do you know anyone in the greater Oconomowoc area that might be interested in our new church? One memorable time I was speaking with a church planter in a community about fifty minutes away. He said he had a couple visit his church from our area that Sunday (they were visiting a family in his church). I called them using that pastor's name and set up an appointment to tell them about our new church. As I was visiting them, I discovered that the young man had grown up in a pastor's family. He left the church after high school, married an unbeliever but was very receptive. Over time, he came back to Christ; his wife came to Christ and was baptized at our first baptism service.

How active are you in getting referrals?

Cold Calling Contacts

New Movers Lists – New Movers Evangelism: www.newmovers.org. Here's how the New Movers Program works: 1) On a monthly basis they furnish names and addresses of new movers in your zip code(s) on peel and stick labels and a manuscript broken down by zip code. 2) They guarantee 100% deliverability of the names you receive. Once you get the newcomers' list you will need to develop a "6 touch" strategy. Here is an example:

- Week 1 - Welcome to the community letter.
- Week 2 - Send a usable gift that newcomers would appreciate.
- Week 3 - Make a phone call to see if they're interested in setting up an appointment to hear more about your new church.
- Week 4 - Write a personal, handwritten note thanking them for the phone conversation or their willingness to meet.
- Week 6-8 - Send an invitation to a special outreach event.
- Week 8 - Add them to your newsletter list.

Phone Book – I know of one church planter who was trying to generate his five contacts a day and out of frustration just grabbed the phone book and called people with a Dutch last name because he was Dutch! Through that simple connection a conversation was started and he would see if they had a spiritual interest. During one of these conversations he saw a woman come to Christ and she eventually became the church's treasurer.

Surveys – Door-to-door surveys on a Saturday work well along with college campus surveys. These can generate a number of contacts. In planting my church I did over three hundred door-to-door opinion poll surveys and over one hundred church name surveys. Not only did I gain great information for reaching our community but I also made strong connections with people. Some of those families are leaders in the church today.

Opinion Poll

OPINION POLL

1. What community sponsored events do you enjoy?

2. What are some of the strengths of this community?

3. What are some of the needs of this community?

4. Do you receive the local newspaper?

5. What type of music do you enjoy listening to? Which stations?

6. Which websites do you most frequently visit?

7. Are you an active member of a local church?

8. Why do you feel most people don't attend church?

9. What topics or current issues do you think the church should be addressing today?

10. What advice would you give to a pastor starting a new church in this area?

11. Would you be interested in receiving more information about this new church?

Name: _____

Address: _____

City: _____ Zip:_____

Phone: _____

Email: _____

College Campus Survey

Getting College Student Contacts
By Andy Sudoff
Associate Pastor of NorthBridge Church, Antioch, IL

What we did at Campus Crusade for Christ in Madison was to set up "Dinner Line Survey" tables. We reserved tables in the lobbies of all of the cafeterias for lunch and dinner times, two days in a row, for a total of four exposure times.

We offered free candy as an attention getter and asked the students to fill out a "30-second survey" for a chance to win $200 at Best Buy.

The survey had these questions:
1. General Info: Name, Dorm & Room #, Phone, male/female, email, year in school.
2. Which of these TV shows best describes your summer: Sports Center, Fear Factor, Cops, Trading Spaces, Family Feud, etc?
3. What I'd most like to find at UW this year: success, opposite sex, good job, myself, good friends, meaning in life.
4. I'd like a free article: (list articles we provide – a good excuse to visit them – something they asked for).
5. Some people think you can know God personally, what do you think? Sure, not a chance, maybe.
6. I'd be interested in how to know God personally: yes, no, worth a try.
7. On a scale of 1-10, how interested are you in info. on small group Bible studies or Christian fellowship available on campus?

This was our main contact generator for the whole year. We actually got bumped out of our table spots last year in the southeast dorms and the campus director said that hurt us for the whole year. So Joe and I adapted this and went to the

College of DuPage (located in West-suburban Chicago). We had free candy and water but didn't do the Best Buy thing and had only a few people stop at our table. The next week we went back with an opportunity to win a $100 Best Buy gift card for filling out a survey, and still offered free candy and water.

Many more people stopped; we got thirty-two surveys filled out and now three people from the college come to our church regularly. We did this in the middle of the summer. We're planning on going back in the fall for the first week of classes for two days from 10 a.m. to 2 p.m. to hopefully get a load of contacts, since many more students will be there.

Here are our adapted survey questions:

   Name, Address, Phone, email
1. What don't you like about church?
2. What would make church better?
3. How would you feel about a pastor who wore jeans and had tattoos?
4. How would you feel about a church that played alternative rock music?
5. How could a church help you specifically?
6. Comments/Questions?

We then called the contacts a few days later to let them know they didn't win (except one guy) and to also take another opportunity to invite them to church. I let them know that if they were not interested that it would be the only call they would receive, they weren't all of a sudden on some crazy church's list of people to call every month.

You can contact Gary Rohrmayer at:

Converge MidAmerica
924 Busse Hwy.
Park Ridge IL 60068

web: www.convergemidamerica.org
email: gary@convergemidamerica.org
blog: www.convergeusa.org

Your Journey Resources
319 Lake Shore Dr.
Lindenhurst IL 60046

www.yourjourney.org
gary@yourjourney.org
www.garyrohrmayer.com

End Notes

CHAPTER 1 END NOTES

[1] Kuhn, Thomas, S., *The Structure of Scientific Revolutions*, Second Edition, Enlarged, The University of Chicago Press, Chicago, 1970 (1962) pg 10
[2] Mittleberg, Mark, *Building a Contagious Church: Revolutionizing The Way We View and Do Evangelism*, Zondervan, Grand Rapids, 2001, pg 400
[3] Simpson, Michael, *Permission Evangelism: When to Talk When to Walk,* David C. Cook, Colorado Springs, CO, 2003

CHAPTER 2 END NOTES

[1] Packer, J.I., *Evangelism and the Sovereignty of God*, Intervarsity Press, Downers Grove, IL, 1961

[2] Hunter, George III, *How to Reach Secular People*, Abingdon Press, Nashville, TN, 1989

[3] Stetzer, Ed; Stanley, Richie; Hayes, Jason, *Lost and Found*, B&H Publishing Group, Nashville, TN, 2009

[4] *Loneliness Is Getting Rampant in America* - http://news.softpedia.com/news/Loneliness-Is-Getting-Rampant-in-America-27518.shtml

CHAPTER 6 END NOTES

[1] Richardson, *Rich Evangelism Out of the Box*, Intervarsity Press, Downers Grove, IL, 2000

[2] Hybels, Bill, *Just Walk Across the Room*, Zondervan, Grand Rapids, MI, 2006

[3] ibid

CHAPTER 7 END NOTES

[1] Hybels, Bill, *Just Walk Across the Room*, Zondervan, Grand Rapids, MI, 2006

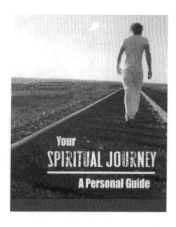

Your Spiritual Journey
By Gary Rohrmayer

Jesus instructed his disciples, "when you enter a house, first say, 'Peace to this house.'" (Luke 10:5) Apparently there was something in the way a person responded to the blessing "Peace to this house" that revealed the level of spiritual receptivity in that house. The author of this guide suggests that we need to find what that statement is for our generation today. From personal experience, he has found that by asking "Do you believe we are on a spiritual journey?" that a person's spiritual receptiveness can often be found.

This guide then asks people where they are on their journey:

- Resisting
- Questioning
- Responding
- Embracing
- Adjusting
- Stabilizing
- Reproducing

This is an excellent spiritual assessment tool for helping spiritual searchers and believers determine where they are spiritually and then showing them how to take the next steps on their spiritual journey. In its ninth printing with over 1.2 million in print.

Retail: $15 per 100 pack
Quantity discounts available

"I have used this tool hundreds of times to start spiritual conversations. This is the most authentic and easy way to engage anyone about the progress they would like to make on their spiritual journey."

– Darryn Scheske
Heartland Church, Fishers, IN

"We love the Spiritual Journey brochure and God is using it for His Glory."

– Debra Webb
CareFirst Pregnancy Crisis Center

www.ChurchSmart.com • 1-800-253-4276